CATHARS

Jean-Paul Laurer

CATHARS

THEIR MYSTERIES AND HISTORY REVEALED

SEAN MARTIN

SHELTER HARBOR PRESS

NEW YORK

Picture Credits
AKG-Images, London   7, 9, 66, 68, 74, 78 Gerard Degeorge, 79 Tristan Lafranchis, 83, 89, 96 Bibliotheque Nationale, Paris, 164 Bibliotheque Nationale, Paris, 101 Gerhard Ruf, 107 Prado, Madrid, 108, 115, 116 Bibliotheque Sainte Genevieve, 153 Neue Pinakothek, Munich, 159 Wittelsbacher Aussleichfonds, Munich, 163 Dusseldorf Museum, 165, 174
British Library/AKG-Images   72/73, 81, 88, 99, 136, 171
Eric Lessing/AKG-Images   31, 102, 123
Herve Champollion/AKG-Images   71, 92, 126, 127, 129, 132, 133
Bridgeman Art Library, London   2/3 and 145 Musee de Augustins, Toulouse, 16 Musee Toulouse-Lautrec, Albi, 50 and 51 Giraudon/Musee Conde, Chantilly, 52 Private Collection, 95 and 100 Archives Charmet/Centre Historiques Archives Nationales, Paris, 103 Santa Maria Novella, Florence, 104 Lauros/Giraudon/Centre Historiques Archives Nationales, Paris, 118 Alinari, San Francesco, Montefalco, 141 AISA/Bibliotheque Nationale, Paris, 142 Bibliotheque Nationale, Paris, 149 Alinari/Museo e Gallerie Nazionali di Capodimonte, Naples
Cameron Collection   11, 30, 35, 47, 93, 124, 146 , 168, 169
Fotolia   29 a4stockphotos, 62 Nougaro, 67 Patrick Pichard, 91 Jean Luc Bohin, 162 Frederic Guillet
Getty-Images, London   12 Bernard Rieger, 17 Altrendo Travel, 23 Sisse Brimberg/National Geographic, 27 Hulton, 32/33 Jeremy Walker/Riser, 54/55 David C Tomlinson, 58 De Agostini Picture Library, 59 M Santini/De Agostini Picture Library, 61 and 74 Roger Viollet Collection, 63 Anton Rivalz/Bridgeman Art Library, 64/65 Travelpix Ltd, 75 Bridgeman Art Library, 76/77 J P de Manne/Robert Harding, 84/85 Peter Adams/The Image Bank, 109 C Sappa/De Agostini Picture Library, 112/113 Travelpix Ltd/The Image Bank, 120/121 Bertrand Gardel/hemis fr, 122 Ruth Tomlinson/Robert Harding World Imagery, 130/131 Musee d'Art et d'Archeologie, Moulins/Bridgeman Art Library, 137 De Agostini Picture Library, 138/139 Philip and Karen Smith/Iconica, 140 Roger Viollet Collection, 143 Bridgeman Art Library, 156 and 157 McDuff Everton/The Image Bank, 173 Marwan Naarmani/AFP
Jupiter Corporation Images   14, 16, 18 The Louvre, Paris, 20, 25, 38, 43, 45, 49, 53, 69, 90, 110/111, 155 National Gallery, London, 166, 167
Private Collections   6 Sanchezn, 13, 15, 19, 22 , 28, 36/37, 39, 40, 41, 42, 70, 86, 97, 119, 105, 125, 150, 151, 154, 161, 172

Cataloging-in-Publication Data has been applied for and may be obtained from the Library of Congress.

Shelter Harbor Press
603 W. 115th Street
Suite 163
New York, NY 10025

ISBN: 978-1-62795-008-4

Printed and bound in Thailand

10 9 8 7 6 5 4 3 2 1

Contents

Foreword

It was the Feast Day of St. Mary Magdalene, July 22nd, 1209, and no massacre had been planned. A French army from the North under the leadership of the papal legate Arnold Amaury was camped outside the town of Béziers in the Languedoc. Recently arrived from a month-long march down the valley of the River Rhône, the army was there to demand the town elders hand over the 222 Cathars—about ten percent of the town's population—that they were known to be harboring. The elders refused—and their refusal was eloquent. It said as much about the complicated political situation in which the Cathars had been able to flourish as it did about the power of the Cathar faith itself.

The Cathars had come to prominence in the Languedoc some 50 years previously, and by the beginning of the thirteenth century Catharism was virtually the dominant religion in

▶ Crusaders attempt to negotiate the handover of 222 heretical Cathars at the gates of Béziers.

◀ Béziers as it is today. This little town was the scene of one of the most horrific massacres in European history.

the Languedoc. Unlike the majority of the Catholic clergy of the time, the Cathars were conspicuously virtuous, living lives of apostolic poverty and simplicity. This in itself would have been enough to get the sect branded as heretics, as happened to the Waldensians in Lyons. What set the Cathars apart, however, was their belief in not one god, but two. According to Cathar theology, there were two eternal principles, good and evil, and the world was under the sway of the latter. The Cathars were also implacably hostile to the Church of Rome, which they denounced vehemently as the Church of Satan.

The Cathars were not the only ones to oppose Rome. Most of what we now think of as the south of France was fiercely independent, and regarded both the northern army and the papal agents as foreign invaders. This made it unthinkable that the Cathars, fellow southerners, could be handed over to the opposition. In the South, the enemy was not heresy, but anyone who challenged the authority and autonomy of the local nobility, the powerful counts and viscounts of Toulouse, Foix, and Carcassonne.

The combination of heresy and politics was a combustible one, however, and Pope Innocent III (1198–1216) saw sufficient grounds to call for a Crusade. The West had been launching Crusades with varying degrees of success since 1095, but they had all been directed against the Muslims. Under Innocent's pontificate, that began to change. The Fourth Crusade, launched in 1202, did not bode well for the heretics and nobles of the Languedoc: Although heading for the Holy Land, the Crusaders veered wildly off target in the spring of 1204 and sacked the Christian city of Constantinople. The campaign waged against the Cathars went further still: It was the first Crusade to be conducted within the West, against people who were fellow countrymen and women.

Arnold Amaury called a meeting with his generals once it became clear that the heretics were not going to be given up without a fight. While this was going on, a fracas broke out between a small band of Crusaders and a group on the walls of the town. Insults were exchanged. In a rash move, the defenders opened the gates and a small group of men from Béziers ventured out to teach the Crusaders a lesson. They swiftly dealt with the northerners, but word spread that the gate was open. Crusaders poured into the town. The news got back to Arnold Amaury. What should he do? How would the army tell the Cathars from the Catholics? The papal legate answered with a paraphrase and a parody of the Biblical phrase "The Lord knoweth them that are his." "Kill them all," said Amaury. "God will recognize his own."

In the ensuing bloodbath of "abattoir Christianity," at least 9,000 people were butchered; some estimates put the figure as high as 15,000 or 20,000. Women and children taking refuge in the Cathedral of St. Nazaire were not spared: The cathedral was torched, and anyone caught fleeing was put to the sword. By the evening, rivers of blood coursed through the streets of Béziers. Churches and houses smoldered. Once they had finished killing, the Crusaders looted what was left of the town.

The Albigensian Crusade, as it came to be known, had begun. Unlike the Fourth Crusade, it had spun out of control at the very beginning. The atrocities of Béziers would have confirmed to Cathars everywhere that the world was indeed evil, and that they alone were God's elect.

▶ Crusaders break into the cathedral at Béziers, killing all those seeking sanctuary inside.

1 Heresy and Orthodoxy

FOLLOWING THE COUNCIL OF NICEA IN A.D. 325, ANY TEACHING THAT DID NOT ACCORD WITH WHAT WAS CONSIDERED TO BE ORTHODOX CHRISTIANITY WAS TO BE BRANDED AS HERESY BY THE CHURCH IN ROME.

Introduction

Catharism was the most popular heresy of the Middle Ages. Indeed, such was its success that the Church and its apologists referred to it as the Great Heresy. At the end of the twelfth century, Catharism was at its zenith: Cathars could be found from Aragon to Flanders, from Naples to the Languedoc. Its equivalent of priests, the Perfect, lived lives so conspicuously virtuous that even their enemies had to admit that they were indeed holy and good people. The Cathars found widespread support in all areas of society, from kings and counts to carpenters and weavers. Women, never welcomed by the Church, became Cathars knowing they could earn respect and actively participate in the faith. This mixture of women, virtue, and apostolic poverty—to say nothing of the Cathar church's popularity—was not appreciated by Rome. Likewise, Rome was not appreciated by the Cathars, who believed that the Church had, in its pursuit of worldly power, betrayed Christ's message.

In some areas of the south of France, Cathars were more numerous than Catholics. It was hardly surprising, then, that the Catholics moved against the Cathars. What shocked contemporaries was not that the Pope ordered a Crusade to put down the heresy, but that the

▶ A knight leads an assorted rabble of Crusaders through the open gates of the city of Béziers.

◀ Bram, a Cathar village in Languedoc, was built in concentric circles as a defensive measure.

Crusaders committed atrocities of the magnitude of Béziers. In the Languedoc, these crimes have never really been forgotten.

Strangely, considering its popularity, the exact origins of Catharism are unknown, but it emerged at a time when the Church, and Europe as a whole, was undergoing enormous changes prior to the emergence of the so-called Renaissance. Although it is now difficult to imagine the scale of an atrocity such as Béziers, we can go some way to understanding the mindset of the Cathars' persecutors by studying the history of the Church, and how heresy emerged from it. Moreover, a study of the history of the dualist heresy—the belief that the devil is as powerful as God, to which Cathars adhered—helps to put the battle between Catholics and Cathars into historical perspective.

Dualism

Dualism existed before Christianity, and may be older than recorded history. The English orientalist Thomas Hyde coined the term in 1700 to describe any religious system that held that God and the devil are two opposing, coeternal principles. The meaning of the term expanded to include any system that revolved around a central, binary pairing (such as the mind/body split in the philosophy of Descartes, or the immortal soul/mortal body in that of Plato). Dualist strands exist in one form or another in all major religions, whether monotheistic (acknowledging one god, such as Islam, Judaism, and Christianity), polytheistic (acknowledging many gods, such as Shintoism and some forms of Wicca, or the pantheon of classical Greece), or monistic (acknowledging that everything—the divine, matter, and humanity—is of one and the same essential substance, such as certain schools of Hinduism, Buddhism, and Taoism). For example, fundamentalist Christianity has a pronounced dualist slant in that it sees many things in the world—rock music, drugs, New Age philosophies, Hollywood blockbusters—as being the work of the devil. Likewise, extremist Islamic groups see non-Muslims as either essentially asleep to the truth, or actively engaged in undermining the religion of the Prophet. In both cases, an "us and them" mentality prevails, from which there is only one escape route (belief in Jesus and Mohammed respectively).

Despite these varying levels of dualism in the different faiths of the world, religious dualism stands apart in positing the notion of the two opposing principles of good and evil. Within the dualist tradition itself, there are generally held to be two schools of thought: Absolute, or radical, dualism; and mitigated, or moderate, dualism. Ugo Bianchi, the Italian historian of religions, identified three distinct features of dualism:

▼ Plato's idea that there is an immortal soul and mortal body lies at the core of dualistic beliefs.

◄ Many religions, including that of Tibetan Buddhists, are dualist in their view of the world.

1. Absolute dualism regards the opposing principles of good and evil as coeternal and equal; mitigated dualism, on the other hand, regards the evil principle as a secondary, lesser power to the good principle.

2. Absolute dualism sees the two principles as locked in combat for all eternity. Many schools regard time as cyclical, so these dualist traditions therefore tend to believe in reincarnation. Mitigated dualism sees historical time as being finite; at the end of time, the evil principle will be defeated by the good.

3. Absolute dualism sees the material world as intrinsically evil, but mitigated dualism regards creation as essentially good.

▲ James the Lesser was the brother of Jesus, and is thought to have been the first leader of the Christian community.

The First Christians

Early Christianity was made up of numerous groups, each with its own beliefs and practices. When the Cathars claimed that they were descended from the first Christians, they probably had in mind the sort of simple Christianity practiced by the Apostles, and they were certainly implying that they were part of the tradition of true Christianity that thrived before the tenets of mainstream Christianity were fixed at the Council of Nicea. The Council, which was convened by the newly converted Emperor Constantine in A.D. 325, not only defined what constituted orthodox Christianity but, in doing so, also defined what was heresy; beliefs of many of the early Christian groups ended up in the latter category. To understand how this came about, it is necessary to consider the fractious political situation in the nascent Church in the first century A.D.

During and immediately after Jesus's ministry, his followers were a minority persecuted by both the Romans and the Pharisees alike. There is continuing controversy as to who was Jesus's successor in the movement. Peter is traditionally seen as the Rock upon which the Church was built, and from which the Roman Catholic Church claims descent, holding Peter as the first Pope. However, it has also been argued that it was Jesus's brother James, known

as James the Lesser, who was the head of the first post-Crucifixion Christian community in Jerusalem. It is thought that James's followers clashed with Paul, Christianity's most fervent missionary. This disagreement becomes all the more significant when one considers that Paul's ideas played a large part—if not the largest—in forming the theology on which the Christian faith is based. Yet he remains a controversial figure: He hardly ever quotes Jesus's words, and his letters—which form the largest part of the New Testament—are often addressed to other Christian communities clarifying points of doctrine or urging them not to stray from the true path. Had early Christianity been a unified movement, there would have been

▼ The baptism of Emperor Constantine led to the adoption of Christianity as the official religion of the Roman Empire.

▶ St. Paul's interpretation of Christianity, here preached at Ephesus, was to become the dominant form of the faith after the Council of Nicea in A.D. 325.

no need for such letters. It would not be going too far to say, as one commentator has done, that "Paul, and not Jesus, was… the Founder of Christianity," and therein lie the origins of Christian heresy: "Paul is, in effect, the first 'Christian' heretic, and his teachings—which became the foundation of later Christianity—are a flagrant deviation from the 'original' or 'pure' form." He is the "first corrupter of the doctrines of Jesus," but he would not be the last. There is a world of difference between the simple but profound Sermon on the Mount preached by Jesus and the doctrine of Christ Crucified preached by Paul.

Gnostic Beliefs Spread

The Jewish Revolt of A.D. 66 destroyed the budding Church of James in Jerusalem, while the Christianity of Paul, who was probably dead or dying in a cell in Rome at that time, would continue to grow. However, Pauline Christianity faced further challenges from the various unorthodox groups that sprang up in the three centuries before the Council of Nicea sat. A number of groups stressed the importance of *gnosis*, or direct experiential knowledge of the divine, and for that reason they are generally known as Gnostics. There is a bewildering number of Gnostic schools

▲ Christ's Sermon on the Mount is often seen as a piece of universal wisdom that transcends religion.

of thought, each with their own, often complicated cosmology, but many of them shared the view that the world was created by an evil demiurge, who was often identified as the God of the Old Testament. Thus they are mitigated, or moderate, dualists. Perhaps the most important Gnostic school was that founded by Marcion in the middle of the second century. Marcion proposed the existence of

▶ God as Creator, as depicted by Michelangelo. This is one of the abiding images of Christian art.

two gods: The true god and the false god; the creator of the material world and the god of the Old Testament. Marcionites rejected the world and were rigorous ascetics. The emerging Roman Church branded Marcion a heretic and condemned his teachings.

The belief in two gods and the asceticism of the Marcionites would later reappear in Catharism, together with another Gnostic idea, that Christ was an apparition rather than a flesh-and-blood human being. Many Gnostics saw Jesus's Passion and Resurrection as essentially ghostly, without any human suffering involved. This idea, which became known as the Docetism, was also pronounced heretical.

Catharism differed from many Gnostic schools of thought in saying that the way to salvation was possible only through the ministrations of the Cathar priesthood, the Perfect, rather than by direct *gnosis* on the part of the believer. It is ironic that in doing so Catharism mirrored Catholicism, which claimed that the only way to salvation was through the intervention of its priests.

The Manicheans

The main heresy the Church had to deal with after Nicea was Manicheism, a syncretistic faith incorporating ideas from Zoroastrianism, Christianity, and Buddhism, which was founded by the Persian prophet Mani (A.D. 216–275).

▼ Manichean priests writing at their desks. Many Manichean texts were written in Sogdian, an Iranian tongue with a rich literature.

There were two distinct classes of Manicheans: The Elect and the Listeners. The Elect were the faith's priesthood, and practiced strict asceticism, abstaining from meat, wine, blasphemy, and sex. The Listeners— the rank-and-file believers—were also expected to observe certain rules, including contributing to the upkeep of the Elect. While they were allowed to own property and marry, they were forbidden to have children. Mani's system was highly complicated, but essentially it was radically dualist: It denied the validity of baptism, held that Christ did not suffer on the cross, rejected the idea of the body as irredeemable, and maintained that the evil principle is the equal of the good.

To the Church, Manicheism was the deadliest of heresies, even worse than Marcionism. However, it enjoyed widespread popularity, and St. Augustine of Hippo was a Listener in the sect for nine years. He later denounced Manicheism in *De Manichaeis* and *De Heresibus*, which were to become the Church's standard reference books on all matters heretical. The Manicheans, increasingly persecuted, fled Europe for Asia.

The Bogomils

The Bogomils, who emerged in the tenth century, were the Cathars' immediate forerunners. Their faith was originally seen as a mixture of Manicheism and Paulicianism, the latter being practiced by a dualist sect that had been active in Bulgaria since the ninth century.

▲ An example of a still-intact Bogomil shrine in Bulgaria.

A Bulgarian priest known as Cosmas denounced the Bogomils in his *Sermon Against the Heretics*, which was written in about A.D. 970. He believed that the sect was founded by a priest named Bogomil, and that its followers rejected the Old Testament and Church sacraments. The only prayer they used was the Lord's Prayer. The Bogomils did not venerate icons or relics, while the cross was denounced as the instrument of Christ's torture. The Church itself was seen as being in league with the devil, whom the Bogomils regarded as the creator of the visible world and as Christ's brother. Their priests were strict ascetics, who abstained from meat, wine, and marriage. The Bogomils were—at least initially—moderate dualists who regarded the devil as a fallen angel, inferior to God. They were well-acquainted with the scriptures, but interpreted them in unorthodox ways, such as identifying the Prodigal Son with Satan. The Bogomil attitude to the Crucifixion was that it was docetic: That is, they regarded it as an apparition, one in which Christ did not really suffer.

The Bogomils had a hierarchy, similar to that of the Manicheans, in which there were the Perfect and the Believers. However, the Bogomils also had Listeners, who were below the Believers. According to the monk Euthymius of Constantinople, who was writing in about

1050, a Bogomil Listener became a Believer by way of a baptism ceremony that included placing the gospel on the initiate's head. The baptism itself was done not with water but by the laying-on of hands. A Believer could become a Perfect only through a course of study, a process that took two years or more to complete. The ceremony in which a Believer became a Perfect was similar to that which made a Listener a Believer, and was known as the *consolamentum* (the consoling), or baptisma.

The Bogomils regarded themselves as being the heirs to true, apostolic Christianity. Modeling himself on Christ and his Apostles, a Bogomil leader had 12 disciples and lived a life of simplicity and poverty, in reaction to what the Bogomils saw as the irredeemable corruption and false teachings of the Church. What worried Euthymius most was that the Bogomils seemed to have created a fully developed counter-church, one whose missionaries were active in spreading the word of the heretical faith. They had reached Sicily by around 1080, and from there began to make inroads into western Europe. The Great Heresy—the biggest threat the medieval church would ever face—had begun.

▼ The Bogomils settled first in the warm valleys of Sicily, and from there spread their teachings into western Europe.

2 The Emergence of the Cathars

AFTER ITS FIRST RECORDED APPEARANCE IN GERMANY IN 1134, THE CATHAR MOVEMENT SPREAD RAPIDLY. IT QUICKLY BECAME ESTABLISHED IN NORTHERN ITALY AND IN THE LANGUEDOC REGION OF SOUTH-WEST FRANCE.

Introduction

Heresy seems to have died down in the second half of the eleventh century. This was possibly related to a program of church reform initiated by Pope Leo IX (1049–1054) and continued by Gregory VII (1073–1085). Gregory's papacy was eventful. His most far-reaching act was to announce that the Church was the only path to God; every other church and faith was anathema. The Church was supreme, according to Gregory, and the Pope himself was the highest possible human authority. Gregory, as the historian Malcolm Lambert notes, "awakened in the laity a new sense of responsibility for reform and a higher expectation of moral standards from their clergy. A genie was unleashed which could never again be put back into its bottle."

The moral life of the clergy became a rallying point for reformers, dissenters, and disaffected churchgoers. In the early years of the twelfth century, this popular reforming zeal became even more strident. Charismatic wandering preachers whipped up parishes and often whole towns into an anticlerical frenzy. Tanchelm of Antwerp, who was active in the Netherlands, inspired such fanatical devotion that his followers were said to drink his bathwater. He did not travel anywhere without an armed guard (a measure that proved futile, as Tanchelm was eventually stabbed by a priest). A rogue Benedictine monk, Henry of Lausanne, caused huge unrest in Le Mans, and effectively ousted the bishop. Peter of Bruys was even more radical, inciting people to break into churches and destroy crucifixes. He held public burnings of crosses until, on Good Friday 1139, a mob threw him onto one of his own bonfires. Arnold of Brescia was yet more extreme than Peter. He launched an attack on Rome in 1146 and declared it a republic. It was not until 1154 that the Pope was able to return to the Vatican. Arnold was burned at the stake; his ashes were scattered in the Tiber to prevent his disciples making them into relics.

However, while the Church was disposing of Arnold in Rome, an even more serious threat appeared far to the north, on the banks of the Rhine.

▶ Pope Gregory is seen here instructing a Benedictine monk to search out heretics.

The First Cathars

The Cathars first appear in the historical record in 1143. Eberwin, the prior of a Premonstratensian house at Steinfeld near Cologne, wrote to the great Cistercian reformer Bernard of Clairvaux that two heretical groups had been uncovered when they had been heard discussing a point of doctrine. These Cathars were brought before the bishop of Cologne for a hearing. It was established that their church was organized in a three-tier system of Elect, Believers, and Listeners. They did not baptize with water but through the laying-on of hands. They condemned marriage, but Eberwin could not find out why "either because they dared not reveal it or, more probably, they did not know." More ominously, the archbishop learned that the heresy "had a very large number of adherents scattered throughout the world" and that it had "lain concealed from the time of the martyrs even to their own day." Most of the heretics were persuaded to recant, although two of their number, apparently a bishop and a deacon, remained unrepentant after three days' intense debate with both clergy and laity. Before the sentence could be pronounced, an angry mob seized the two heretics and threw them onto a fire.

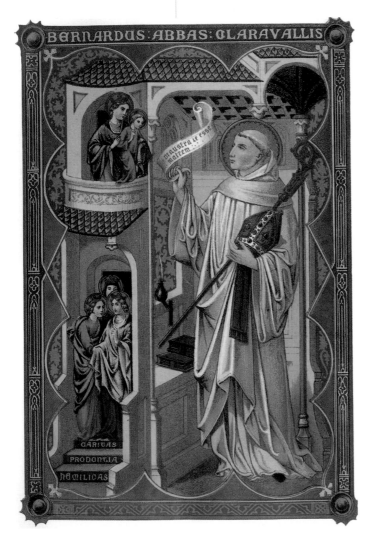

▼ St. Bernard of Clairvaux, the influential French cleric, was highly critical of all forms of heresy.

What was different about this new heresy was that it was not merely anticlericalism of the sort propagated by Henry of Lausanne and the motley assortment of libertarian preachers who had been such a colorful feature of religious life during the twelfth century up to that point. These new heretics had organized themselves properly. Indeed, the two groups discovered at Cologne were not merely dissenters from Catholicism,

▲ The Cathars first established themselves in Cologne, where their numbers grew fast, much to the dismay of the Church.

they were members of an underground church that had had time to build itself up and put itself in direct opposition to Rome and all that it stood for. As Malcolm Lambert puts it, the Cathars "offered a direct, headlong challenge to the Catholic Church, which is dismissed outright as the Church of Satan."

Nothing like this had ever happened before, and suddenly the new heresy seemed to be everywhere. Its rise concerned no less a churchman than Bernard of Clairvaux, who, after receiving Eberwin's letter about events in the Rhineland, composed two sermons denouncing the heretics. He equated the heretics with the "little foxes" in the Song of Songs 2:15: "Catch the foxes, the little foxes, before they ruin our vineyard in bloom." Bernard's tracts are full of the standard accusations: He warns of the heretics' cunning and secrecy, and accuses them of sexual misconduct and aberration. As to what could be done about the situation, he comes close to condemning the burghers of Cologne who had cast their Cathars into the flames: "Their zeal [in rooting out heresy] we approve, but

▲ The city of Cologne witnessed the beginnings of the persecution of the Cathars. A mob there seized two adherents of the faith and burned them alive.

we do not advise the imitation of their action, because faith is to be produced by persuasion, not imposed by force." He goes on to add, however, that "it would, without a doubt, be better that they should be coerced by the sword of him "who beareth not the sword in vain' than that they should be allowed to draw away many other persons into their error." In other words, he could tolerate people being quietly heretical at home, but they could not be allowed to seek out converts. As for punishment, the worst thing he advises is expulsion from the Church. In light of what was to happen in the Languedoc in the early years of the following century, Bernard's views are remarkably humane and tolerant. If the Church had followed his lead—he was after all the most powerful figure in the Church of his time—then history might have been different.

A Decisive Approach

Bernard himself visited the Languedoc in 1145, suspicious that the count of Toulouse, Alfonso-Jordan, was not doing enough to check the growth of heresy in his lands. Whether Bernard's visit happened before or after he composed his brace of antiheretical sermons, we do not know. What we do know, however, is that the man famed for his preaching skills met a decidedly mixed reaction. He got off to a good start in Albi. The papal legate there was not the most popular of people, and Bernard knew he had to make his words count. His sermon attacked Henry of Lausanne, who was then in the Albi area and was known to have supporters there. It was a rousing performance. Concluding his sermon, Bernard asked all those in the congregation who accepted the Catholic Church to raise their right hand. Everyone put up their hand. The moment marked the end of Henry's support in the Languedoc.

◄ Bernard of Clairvaux in the act of exorcising the devil from a heretic.

▶ Next page: Minerve, Herault, is a typical hilltop town in the rolling Languedoc countryside.

A Land of Heresy

Events in the village of Verfeil to the north-east of Toulouse made Bernard realize that other forms of heresy were still very much alive. He preached in the church there, but when he tried to deliver another sermon outside the church, his words were rendered inaudible by local knights, who deliberately rapped their swords on their shields to drown out his voice. Bernard was humiliated, and he was laughed out of town.

The incident could be ascribed as much to anticlericalism, which was rife in the South at the time, as to heresy, but to Bernard there was only one explanation. He returned fuming to his monastery in Champagne, declaring the whole of the Languedoc to be "a land of many heresies" that needed "a great deal of preaching."

The great deal of preaching urged by Bernard was largely unforthcoming. Christendom had more pressing matters to deal with in the shape of the Second Crusade, with Bernard himself taking an active role in its early stages. However, once the Crusade was on its way to the East the Pope, Eugenius III, did try to do something about the growth of heresy: He issued a papal bull in 1148 forbidding anyone to help heretics in Gascony, Provence, and elsewhere. In 1157, the Archbishop of Rheims presided over a meeting of the provincial council, which condemned a group of heretics called Piphles who rejected marriage. At the Council of Tours in 1163, Pope Alexander III presided over a gathering of cardinals and bishops who reiterated Eugenius's directives by passing legislation directed against "Albigensians," so-called because the Great Heresy was flourishing unchecked in the town of Albi, and those who helped them. The same year, Hildegard of Bingen had an apocalyptic vision in which she saw the emergence of the Cathars as evidence that the devil had been released from the bottomless pit. Only destruction could now come to mankind.

▶ Hildegard of Bingen had a nightmarish vision of the Cathars' emergence. It was taken by the Church as a sign from God.

The Living Icons

The Cathars, or Good Christians as they called themselves, must have been horrified to learn the things that were being said of them. The rumors that they were participants in satanic ceremonies were no more than the product of the imaginations of their critics. The Church was keen to paint heretics of all denominations in the blackest possible colors, and in doing so they frequently resorted to cliché and outright fabrication. The Jews, for example, were said to steal Christian children and sacrifice them in secret. As for the Cathars, they were far from satanic. Many of their contemporaries regarded them as better Christians than the Catholics, a fact that the Church was later forced to acknowledge.

Their virtue was not the only thing that set them apart; the Cathars' beliefs further removed them from the mainstream of Christian life. They inherited much of their doctrine from the Bogomils. Catharism was dualist, holding that the material world is evil and the creation of the devil himself. The true god existed in a world of eternal light beyond the dark abyss of human existence. Both the Cathars and the Bogomils rejected the Church and all its sacraments. The only sacrament they observed was the *consolamentum*, which was a form of baptism and, if administered on the deathbed, extreme unction.

▼ At the Last Supper, Christ said of the bread and wine: "This is my body, this is my blood." The Cathars, like many present-day Christians, believed that these words were meant only as a metaphor.

▼ Both the Bogomils and the Cathars rejected the image of the cross which they regarded as an instrument of torture.

The only prayer both churches used was the Lord's Prayer, with the Cathars substituting the phrase "supersubstantial bread" for "daily bread." Bogomils and Cathars alike dismissed most of the Old Testament—and its belligerent deity—as satanic. Both movements regarded the entity of the Church—Catholic in the West, Orthodox in the East—as the Church of Satan, and rejected it utterly. Church buildings—the churches, chapels, and cathedrals themselves—were likewise seen as no more holy than any other building; neither sect built places of worship, preferring instead to meet in people's homes, or in barns or fields. Antidualist propaganda produced at the time tells of a Bogomil monk who feigned orthodoxy and built a church on the banks of the Bosphorus, putting a latrine behind the altar in order to desecrate it. Similarly, in Toulouse, a Cathar was said to have entered a local church and emptied his bowels on the altar, cleaning himself up with the altar cloth.

In both faiths the cross was seen as the instrument of Christ's torture; Bogomils and Cathars refused to venerate it. They interpreted the Eucharist allegorically, and took the docetic line on Christ's nature, his miracles, Passion, and Resurrection, believing them to be no more than apparitions. Cathars and Bogomils regarded marriage as fornication, and saw it as a means by which souls became entrapped in the material world through the thoroughly distasteful business of childbirth. While there is little or no evidence concerning the role of women in the Bogomil church, the Cathars regarded women as the equal of men, and Catharism offered women the chance to participate fully in the faith at all levels.

The structure of the Cathar church was derived from the Bogomil model. Cathars were divided into three classes: Listeners, Believers, and the Perfect. The Listeners were people who chose not to commit to the faith wholeheartedly; they might hear the occasional sermon, but no more. At this stage, Listeners would hear sermons that were close in spirit to those of evangelical Christianity. If they chose to become Believers, they would be asked to participate in a ceremony known as the *convenanza*, which formally bound them to the Cathar church. Believers formed the majority of the movement. They were ordinary men and women who had ordinary jobs and who lived in towns or villages. They did not lead lives of monastic seclusion, and they did not have to abstain from meat, wine, or sex. Instead they were very much involved in the world of matter. They were taught to be in the world but not of it, to follow the basic teachings of the Gospels, to love one another, to live a life of faith, and to seek God. Believers were not exposed to dualist doctrine, which was usually reserved for the ears of the Perfect alone. The Perfect were the austere, top-level Cathars who were effectively the movement's priesthood. In both the Cathar and the Bogomil faith, the Perfect were held in the highest regard: They were seen as embodying the Holy Spirit, being the living church itself. They were nothing less than living icons.

▲ The vast majority of Cathars lived the lives of ordinary people and were not required to deny themselves worldly pleasures.

▶ The idea of repentance, as expounded in Matthew's Gospel was a central tenet of Catharism.

The *Consolamentum*

Central to Catharism was the baptismal rite known as the *consolamentum*. It was the means by which a Believer could become a Perfect, and thereby attain salvation. Without it, the Believer would be condemned to remain in the world of matter in their next incarnation. The *consolamentum* survives in two versions, one written in Latin and dating from 1235–1250, and one in Occitan (the language of the Languedoc) which dates from the late 1200s, although both were probably based on one twelfth-century Latin original. According to these documents, the ceremony, led by a Cathar elder, began with a blessing, which was followed by a recitation of the Lord's Prayer, in which the words "supersubstantial bread" replaced the more usual "daily bread." The elder read from the first 17 verses of St. John's Gospel, which was then—according to the Occitan version—followed by a series of requests for forgiveness. The

▼ The Lord's Prayer as spoken by the Cathars was more reminiscent of present-day wording than that which was current at the time.

elder placed the Book—either the New Testament or St. John's Gospel—on a table covered with a cloth, and explained in detail to the Believer the import of what he or she was about to do; a line-by-line exegesis of the Lord's Prayer then followed. The elder reminded the supplicant of the need for repentance, citing Matthew 6.15, "But if ye will not forgive men their trespasses, no more shall your father forgive your trespasses."

Sometimes there was a break in the ceremony at this point, but this was not mandatory. What followed next was the *consolamentum* itself. The elder announced that the baptism the supplicant was about to receive by the laying-on of hands had been preserved "from the time of the apostles until

this time and it has passed from Good Men to Good Men until the present moment, and it will continue to do so until the end of the world." The Believer was urged to keep Christ's commandments to the utmost of his or her ability, and was told not commit adultery, kill, lie, swear an oath, nor steal. They were to turn the other cheek toward all who persecuted them, and were expected to hate this world and the things of this world. The Believer pledged to do these things and gave the elder the *melioramentum*, or ritual greeting by which Believers honored the Perfect. The elder then took the Holy Book from the table and placed it on the Believer's head. All the Perfect present then placed their right hand on the Believer. The ceremony ended with further requests for forgiveness, and a ritual known as the Act of Peace, in which all present kissed each other on the cheek, and also kissed the Book. The Believer was now "consoled." He or she had become a Perfect.

▼ Despite its strong defenses and inaccessible location, the castle of Quéribus changed hands several times during the Cathar wars.

The Life of a Perfect

The new Perfect would be expected to keep the vows for the rest of his or her life. The slightest slip would necessitate a new consoling, and also invalidate any *consolamentums* that he or she had administered: The slip was known euphemistically as "making a bad end." The duties of a Perfect were rigorous. They were expected to pray 15 times a day, and to fast on Mondays, Wednesdays, and Fridays. Prayers were to be said on horseback, when crossing rivers, and when entering the homes of Believers. If the Perfect—who usually traveled in pairs—came across goods belonging to someone, they were only to return them if they were sure the goods could be reunited with their rightful owner. If not, then the Perfect were instructed to leave the goods where they found them. If they happened upon a bird or animal caught in a trap, they were to release the bird or animal on condition that they were able to recompense the hunter with money or a gift. When visiting Believers, they were expected to bless them and their food if they were dining together, and to leave a small gift in payment. Many Believers waited until they were close to death to take the *consolamentum*, in which case, the cloth and Book would be laid on the Believer's bed. If the Believer subsequently recovered, he or she was usually advised to seek reconsoling at a later date.

Once a month, all the Perfect in a given area would gather to meet their deacon and confess their sins, a ceremony known as the *apparellamentum*. Three times a year, the Perfect were expected to undertake 40-day fasts, mirroring Christ's experiences in the wilderness: From November 13th to Christmas Eve; from Quinquagesima Sunday (the Sunday before Ash Wednesday) to Easter; and from Pentecost to the Feast of the Apostles Peter and Paul on June 29th. The Perfect were notable for the way that they dressed as well as for their rigorous observances: They wore black robes with a cord tied round the waist.

▲ The Cathar Perfect observed a strict code of conduct when traveling. They were obliged to act with generosity to all with whom they came into contact.

3 The Spread of Catharism

THE APPEAL OF CATHARISM WAS AS INSTANT AS IT WAS PROFOUND. THE CATHAR FAITH UNDERMINED THE AUTHORITY OF THE CATHOLIC CHURCH BY OFFERING WHAT SEEMED TO BE A GENTLER, MORE BENIGN VERSION OF CHRISTIANITY.

Et auci
ennes hi
stoires de
eut que
eracles
qui mlt
fu bons z
crestiens

Ourertoit
lempire de
ronme.ap
en son temp
a vabome
auoit ia est
te qui fu
meffages

b diabl
il fift en
dunt q
estoit p
phetes
nouos z
medie
temps

Introduction

By the time the Church became aware of the Cathars, two things were apparent: Catharism was already a fully fledged church; and the Cathars—along with fellow-travelers such as the Publicans and the Waldensians—seemed to be everywhere. Their ideas looked like a threat to the Church, and to Christian society generally. In 1163, more Cathars were unearthed in Cologne; they went to the stake like their coreligionists had done 20 years before. In England, a group known as Publicans—who may have been Cathars under another name—preached at Canterbury and Oxford, hoping to win new converts. They were denounced, branded, and thrown out into the winter snow. People were forbidden to help them or to give them shelter. All of the Publicans died of exposure.

In 1165, a group of Cathars came to light in Lombers, a town ten miles (16 kilometers) to the south of Albi. The Church took the threat of these Cathars very seriously. The heretics were arraigned before six bishops, eight abbots, the local viscount, and Constance, sister to the King of France and wife to Raymond V, count of Toulouse. The Cathars themselves must have known that they had to be careful; word that their brethren in Germany had been burned for their beliefs would no doubt have reached them. Led by a Perfect called Olivier, the Cathars at Lombers engaged in debate with the clergy. They answered questions astutely, referring frequently to the New Testament. However, they could not dissemble on the issue of oath-taking: This was something that Cathars would not do under any circumstances. They claimed Biblical authority, citing Matthew 5.33–37: "But I say unto you, swear not at all: Neither by heaven, for it is God's seat: Nor yet by the earth, for it is his footstool: Neither by Jerusalem, for it is the city of that great king… your communication shall be yea, yea: Nay, nay. For whatsoever is more than that, cometh of evil." In medieval society, the swearing of oaths was the standard way of sealing an agreement, between lord and vassal, between Church and state. It was the closest thing the Middle Ages had to a legally binding contract, and to refuse to swear an oath was an act of the greatest subversion. Olivier and his fellow Cathars launched a scathing attack on the Church, denouncing it as hypocritical and accusing the assembled bishops of being little better than ravening wolves. Despite this, the Lombers Cathars were allowed to remain at large. Anticlerical feeling was rife in the Languedoc, and there were no doubt many people at Lombers that day who, while not necessarily supporting the Cathars in their beliefs, were unwilling to see them burned. Such apparent toleration of heresy did not go unnoticed, and stored up trouble for the future.

◄ A seventeenth-century engraving shows the mass burning of Cathars in Cologne in 1163.

The Council of St. Félix

The theological debate at Lombers was a small gathering compared to the congress of Cathars that took place two years later in the village of St Félix de Caraman in the Lauragais, south of Toulouse. This later meeting has been called "the most imposing gathering ever recorded in the history of the Cathars." It was, in effect, an international symposium of Cathars from all over Europe, including—crucially—a delegation from the East. The purpose of the meeting seems initially to have been to reorganize the Cathar church, and to decide on important issues such as the creation of new bishoprics, the demarcation of diocesan boundaries, and the appointment of new bishops.

Presiding over the council was the enigmatic figure of Papa Nicetas. He had traveled to the Languedoc from Lombardy, and was treated with the utmost respect. The word *papa* is Latin for pope, but it is not certain whether he was one of the heretical Balkan antipopes so feared by the Church. In all probability, he was a bishop of the Bogomil church in Constantinople, although it has also been suggested that he was a charismatic preacher fulfilling the western hunger for eastern wisdom. He may have been both. What is known for sure, however, is that Nicetas effected a profound shift in Languedocian Catharism; he changed the nature of the movement forever.

If it is the case that a Bogomil bishop chaired an important Cathar gathering, then this amounts to the first concrete evidence we have of a connection between the two heresies. While they shared numerous beliefs and practices, there is no evidence to link the Bogomil faith and Catharism prior to the meeting at St Félix. "As far as extant records are concerned," writes Malcolm Lambert, "no Bogomil was ever caught preaching [in the West], leading a group of neophytes

► Crusader knights returning from the Holy Land brought back many new ideas. Some knights may have encountered Byzantine monks who were Bogomils, and been influenced by their beliefs.

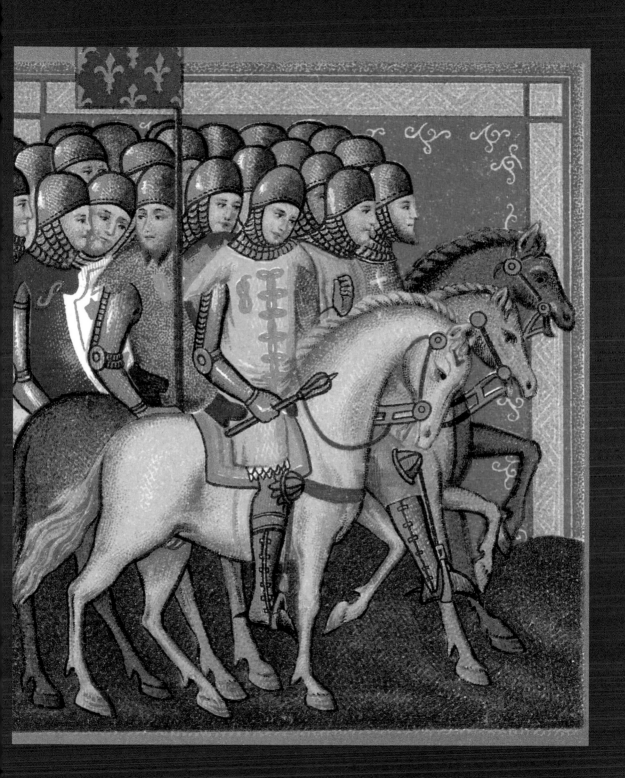

or disseminating literature." Quite how the Bogomils spread their dualist creed in the West therefore remains a mystery. One suggestion is that the heretical Byzantine monks could have spread Bogomilism while on pilgrimages to shrines in the West, although where they could have made their first landfall is open to conjecture. Palermo in Sicily seems to have had a Bogomil presence by about 1082: Possibly this group was made up of refugees from persecution. Bogomilism may have found another route into Europe via returning Crusaders, some of whom could have adopted the faith while campaigning in the East. We do not know for sure. The Bogomils remain among the most elusive of all medieval sects, and the lack of firm evidence about their activities in the West gives them the air of phantoms.

Catharism must surely have been developing for some decades before the events of 1143 brought it to the notice of the authorities. Despite its Bogomil ancestry, it was, as one commentator has noted, "never subservient to the East: As soon as we have records of its existence, it is unmistakably and thoroughly westernized and develops a life of its own." The Cathar faith as Nicetas encountered it in 1167 was rapidly expanding, and the meeting at St Félix provided the opportunity to impose some order on the organization. The rambling diocese of Toulouse was split: Toulouse, Carcassonne, and either Agen or Val d'Aran became bishoprics, and the border between Toulouse and Carcassonne was settled. One aspect of the Cathar church that remained unchanged, however, was the process by which bishops were elected. Each Cathar bishop had to have two bishops-in-waiting beneath him; they were known as the *filius major* and *filius minor* (elder son and younger son). When the bishop died, retired, or resigned, the *filius major* automatically became the next bishop, and the *filius minor* became the *filius major*. A new younger son was then chosen. This system helped maintain the unity of the Cathar church, and, in the case of the Languedocian church, helped both to unify and strengthen it. In the Cathar church, unlike in the Catholic one, there were no protracted rows about succession and election.

The Proceedings at St Félix

At some point in the proceedings at St Félix, Nicetas delivered a bombshell. The Cathars of the Languedoc were derived from the *ordo*—or rule—of the Bulgarian church, who were moderate dualists.

▼ Heretical texts, like the heretics themselves, were tested by fire. It was said that a "good book" thrown on a fire would float away, while an evil one would surely burn.

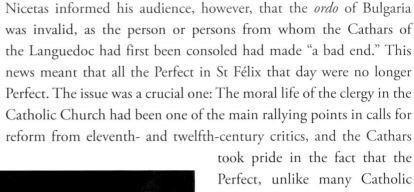

Nicetas informed his audience, however, that the *ordo* of Bulgaria was invalid, as the person or persons from whom the Cathars of the Languedoc had first been consoled had made "a bad end." This news meant that all the Perfect in St Félix that day were no longer Perfect. The issue was a crucial one: The moral life of the clergy in the Catholic Church had been one of the main rallying points in calls for reform from eleventh- and twelfth-century critics, and the Cathars took pride in the fact that the Perfect, unlike many Catholic priests, were actually holy; they practiced what they preached. To have the Perfect who consoled you be exposed as sinful—even if it were only through a minor indiscretion—meant having to be reconsoled.

▼ When Nicetas of Constantinople coopted the French Cathars to the *ordo* of Drugunthia, he set them on a collision course with the Roman Catholic Church.

Nicetas had a solution to the problem. His church in Constantinople lived by the *ordo* of the church of Drugunthia, and he proposed that everyone accept the new *ordo*. There was one crucial difference between the churches of Bulgaria and Drugunthia: The latter were absolute dualists who were, in the eyes of Rome, even more dangerously heretical than the moderates. After some debate among themselves, the delegates at St Félix chose to accept the *ordo* of Drugunthia.

Catharism in Italy

Nicetas traveled to St Félix in the company of Italian Cathars. In Italy, as elsewhere in Europe, anticlericalism was rife. Arnold of Brescia's campaigns against the Pope ended with Arnold's execution in 1155, but stability did not return to the Italian peninsula. The papacy remained locked in conflict with the Holy Roman Emperor, the formidable Frederick Barbarossa, and with a series of imperially sponsored antipopes. The situation was exacerbated by the influence of the Pataria, a group of pro-reform clergy who opposed the abuses of a mainly aristocratic clergy during the pontificate of Gregory VII. Like their brethren north of the Alps, the Pataria called for a morally pure clergy and remained deeply suspicious of conspicuous wealth and privilege among churchmen. The Pataria remained popular even after the movement's dissolution, and the time seemed ripe for someone to take on the mantle of Arnold of Brescia.

According to the thirteenth-century inquisitor and chronicler Anselm of Alessandria, Catharism came to Italy from northern France. Some time in the 1160s, a "certain notary" from that area encountered a gravedigger by the name of Mark in Concorezzo, to the north-east of Milan. Mark, evidently enthused by what the French notary had told him of the new faith, spread the word to his friends John Judeus, who was a weaver, and Joseph, who worked as a smith. Soon there was a small group of would-be Cathars in Milan, and they asked the notary from France for further instruction in the faith. They were told to go to Roccavione, a village on the road that led over the Alpes Maritimes to Nice, where a group of Cathars from northern France who followed the *ordo* of Bulgaria had established a small community. Mark received the *consolamentum* and returned to

▲ The Holy Roman Emperor Frederick Barbarossa was at logger-heads with the Church throughout the papacy of Gregory VII.

▶ Next page: Scaligers Castle, a Cathar stronghold in Malcesine, Veneto in Italy.

Concorezzo, where he founded a Cathar church and began to preach. Gathering followers, Mark spread the word in both the March of Treviso and in Tuscany. It is probable that John Judeus and Joseph the smith also received the *consolamentum*, and began preaching careers. Further Cathar churches were established in the March of Treviso (it was also known as the church of Vicenza), at Desenzano, Florence, Val del Spoleto, and Bagnolo (sometimes known as the church of Mantua, which was nearby).

Nicetas's appearance some time prior to the gathering at St Félix changed the situation in Italy. Unlike in the Languedoc, where his mission had a unifying effect, his presence here was divisive. As at St Félix, Nicetas told Mark and his group that the *consolamentum* they

had received had been rendered invalid—presumably because the Perfect who had administered it had come to a bad end. Nicetas duly reconsoled Mark and his colleagues, and the group then accompanied Nicetas on his historic trip to the Languedoc. After the gathering at St Félix, Nicetas disappeared; probably he returned to Constantinople. In his place another eastern bishop, Petracius, arrived from the church of Bulgaria. He informed Mark that Simon, the Drugunthian bishop who had consoled Nicetas, had been caught with a woman and was also guilty of other unspecified immoralities. (Others believe that it was Nicetas himself who had made a bad end—which, if true, lends weight to the theory that he was something of a charlatan.) Mark and his group were left with no choice: They had to be reconsoled for a second time.

Mark set off for the East, determined to seek a valid reconsoling. On his return, but before he reached Concorezzo, he was thrown into prison. John Judeus managed to speak with Mark in prison, and was reconsoled by him. John Judeus did not have the support of all the Italian Cathars, some of whom formed a breakaway group under Peter of Florence. An attempt to broker a peace between the two factions was made. Delegates from both sides went to the bishop of the northern French Cathars, from whom all the Italians had originated, to seek arbitration. The bishop declared that the matter should be settled by the drawing of lots. There was a Biblical precedent for this: In the Acts of the Apostles it is written that the disciples drew lots to elect Judas's successor. The winning candidate should go to the East, be reconsoled, then return to Italy and proceed to reunify the Cathar church. The plan was scuppered by Peter of Florence, who, in a fit of pique, declared that he would not submit to the drawing of lots. This lost him support and John Judeus became the winning candidate for the journey to the East. However, some of Peter's party continued to protest. John Judeus resigned, not wishing to cause further trouble.

▲ Mosio, where a council was convened to heal the differences between the two opposing Cathar factions. It is located in the area between Mantua and Cremona in the north of Italy.

A Fragile Peace is Broken

In an attempt to sort out the situation, a council was convened at Mosio, which lay between Mantua and Cremona. The new plan was that each side would propose a candidate from the rival group. The chosen candidates were Garattus, from John Judeus's party, and John de Judice from Peter's. Again deferring to the apostolic precedent, lots were drawn and Garattus was chosen. Plans were laid for his journey to the East: He started to choose traveling companions, and money was collected for the trip. However, just as Garattus and his party were about to depart, two informers claimed that he had been with a woman. The fragile peace was broken, and Italian Catharism splintered permanently. Desenzano remained faithful to the *ordo* of Drugunthia—and therefore Nicetas—and became a stronghold of absolute dualism. Meanwhile, Concorezzo, the church of Mark the gravedigger, reverted to the *ordo* of Bulgaria and moderate dualism. The church in the March of Treviso took the middle line, and sent its candidate to *Ecclesia Sclavoniae*, which was impartial in the dispute between the churches of Bulgaria and Drugunthia. Unlike their counterparts in the Languedoc, the Italian churches would continue to bicker for the rest of the movement's existence.

▼ Treviso in Italy, where the Cathars took a middle line between the teachings of the churches of Bulgaria and Drugunthia.

4 Persecution

CATHARISM BECAME FIRMLY ESTABLISHED IN THE LANGUEDOC IN THE COURSE OF THE TWELFTH CENTURY. BY THE TIME POPE INNOCENT III CAME TO THE THRONE IN 1198, IT WAS CLEAR TO THE CHURCH THAT THE ALBIGENSIAN HERESY WOULD HAVE TO BE TORN OUT BY ITS VERY ROOTS.

Introduction

The Languedoc in the year 1200 was a prosperous region. It was one of the most cosmopolitan and sophisticated areas of Europe. Trade flourished in the great towns of Toulouse and Carcassonne, and Toulouse itself was outshone only by Rome and Venice in terms of size and cultural life. The arts were enjoying a renascence, with the ideals of courtly love being praised in the songs and poems of the troubadours. Religious tolerance was conspicuous, and Jews in particular enjoyed freedoms that they were denied elsewhere. Catharism was part of this rich social fabric; by the turn of the thirteenth century, the faith was endemic throughout the Languedoc. Encouraged by the momentous visit of Nicetas, the Perfect had been hard at work for more than a generation, spreading the dualist word throughout the South and creating a heretical kingdom that stretched from Provence to Aragon. Their success was a tribute not only to the courage and faith of the Perfect, but also to the unique way of

▼ Toulouse was a city of major influence and culture during the Cathar era, outclassed only by Rome and Venice.

life that the Languedoc was enjoying at this high-water mark in its history. The name Languedoc comes from the phrase *langue d'oc,* the "language of yes," a reference to the fact that in the region's native tongue, Occitan, the word for yes was *oc,* not *oui.* The French language and those who spoke it were far to the north in the Île de France. Power in the Languedoc was shared between the counts of Toulouse, Foix, and Comminges, and the viscount of Béziers and Carcassonne. Although the Languedocian Cathars did not argue among themselves, the lords

of Languedoc resembled the Italian Cathars: Disputes were frequent, quarrels habitual, petty vendettas the norm.

The most powerful of them all was Raymond VI, count of Toulouse. His court was a heterogeneous mix of Catholics, Cathars, and Jews, entertained by troubadours and jongleurs. His friends, as the historian Stephen O'Shea notes, "were not distinguished for their piety." Raymond had inherited his title in 1194 from his father, Raymond V. His parents seem to have had opposing views on the matter of faith: Raymond's mother, Constance, had been present at Lombers in 1165 when the Cathars had faced down their Catholic opponents, while his father had invited a group of churchmen to investigate heresy in his lands in 1177. Then, the churchmen had concluded that eradicating Catharism from the Languedoc was an impossible task. The one man whom they did manage to convict was sent to Jerusalem as penance. When he got back to Toulouse, he was given a hero's welcome and a well-paid job. As St. Bernard had found, the Languedoc was indeed a "land of many heresies," and respect for the Church was as low as it could possibly be.

◄ Previous page: The Languedoc countyside remains much as it was in the Cathar era, and many of the historic sites of the period are still to be found.

▼ Troubadours, singers of love songs, were a dubiously secular institution in a religious age. Their performances were a feature of court life under Raymond VI.

A Church in Retreat

During Raymond VI's early years as count of Toulouse, the clergy were deeply unpopular. They were conspicuously indulgent, and there were churches where Mass had not been said in years. The locals used the phrase "I'd rather be a priest" when declining to perform some unpleasant task. The bishop of Toulouse, Raymond of Rabastens, was particularly notorious. His main claim to fame seems to have been mortgaging church property in order to hire mercenaries and conduct a private war against his own vassals. Raymond duly bankrupted the diocese. He was replaced with the more able Fulk of Marseilles, who had been a former troubadour and was thought to be the only man who could handle the hornet's nest of the Languedoc. Such was the dire state of diocesan finances that when Fulk took over he dared not send his mules to the well for water lest they be repossessed.

Interference from the nobility served to undermine the Church still further. The activities of the Trencavels—rivals to Raymond VI's family, the St Gilles—are a case in point. In 1178, they had the bishop of Albi arrested on trumped-up charges and thrown into jail; the following year they forced an enormous sum of money out of the coffers of the monastery of St Pons-de-Thomières. In 1197, they contested the election of a new abbot in Alet, in the highlands of the Languedoc. Their intermediary in the dispute, Bertrand de Saissac (several of whose family were Perfect) dug up the body of the former abbot, propped him up in a chair, and asked him who should be his successor. When a Trencavel puppet was installed, the late abbot was returned to his resting place.

In the midst of all this chaos, the Cathars were quietly spreading word of their faith. While the likes of Raymond VI and the Trencavels were priest-baiting or conducting territorial wars against fellow nobles, the Good Christians were establishing themselves in home and hearth the length and breadth of the Languedoc. Part of their success had to do with the respect they showed to women, who enjoyed a higher status in the Languedoc than in most other parts of Europe. Primogeniture was nonexistent, estates being shared between sons and daughters. Although men were the largest landowners, women were able to own property and thereby increase their status in society. Similarly, the Cathars saw the sexes as equal, and there was nothing to stop a woman becoming a Perfect. So it is not surprising that women responded to Catharism, given that the faith actively encouraged their participation, and offered them the possibility of becoming Perfect and therefore semidivine. The Catholic Church offered no such respect. If you were a woman in the Languedoc of 1200, it made more sense to be a Cathar than a Catholic, with the result that women played a crucial role in helping the faith establish a network of Cathar houses across the Languedoc. Some of them, such as the houses at Laurac and Villemur, were exclusively for women.

▼ The church of Mary Magdalene still dominates the skyline in Albi, one of the major centers of Catharism.

▲ Innocent III, who became Pope in
1198, was determined to do better
than his predecessors, and to deal

Innocent III

The appointment of Fulk of Marseilles to the destitute bishopric of Toulouse was part of a wider plan of reform initiated by the new Pope, Innocent III. Born Lotario dei Conti di Segni in 1160, Innocent studied theology in Paris and law in Bologna before taking the cloth. He rose rapidly through the Church hierarchy and was crowned Pope on February 22nd, 1198. His appointment came at the end of a disastrous century for the Church: Of the 16 Popes who ruled in the twelfth century, 11 had ended their pontificates in places other than Rome, which was barred to them by Arnold of Brescia, rioters, and foreign kings. The papacy was also in constant dispute with the rulers of the Holy Roman Empire. Frederick Barbarossa in particular had been a thorn in Rome's side for much of his reign, which had ended when he drowned crossing a river during the Third Crusade. Innocent was well aware of the troubles his predecessors had endured, and was determined to prevent history from repeating itself.

▼ Frederick Barbarossa, Holy Roman Emperor, is depicted drowning as he crosses a river on the way back from the Crusades.

Dealing with the situation in the Languedoc was a high priority for Innocent from the beginning. There had been periodic attempts to tackle heresy before his accession. Aside from the delegation that had responded to Raymond V's invitation in 1177, the Third Lateran Council of 1179 had debated the issue of heresy, and decreed that force could be used to destroy it. Two years later, Henri de Marcy besieged Lavaur, where two Cathars were known to be hiding. The town surrendered and handed over the Cathars, who were persuaded to return to the Church; they became

► The fall of Jerusalem to Saladin was a disaster that preoccupied the Church totally. So for a time the Cathars were left in peace.

canons in Toulouse. Of greater significance was the papal bull *Ad abolendam*, issued by Pope Lucius III in 1184. Although it was as much concerned with Italy as the Languedoc, it was the first direct attempt to deal directly with the problem of heresy. It denounced various sects—including the Cathars—and instructed clergy to make annual visits to parishes where heresy was suspected. However, Christendom had more pressing matters to deal with. The situation in the Latin East was deteriorating, and in 1187 it was overrun by Saladin's forces. Jerusalem fell to a Muslim army on October 2nd of that year. By comparison with this disaster, heresy at home seemed to be a matter of little consequence.

Nevertheless Innocent realized that action had to be taken at once to prevent the already bad situation in the Languedoc from getting worse. In one letter, he described the clergy of Narbonne as "blind men, dumb dogs who can no longer bark… men who will do anything for money… zealous in avarice, lovers of gifts, seekers of rewards." There was no doubt in Innocent's mind as to who was the biggest offender: "The chief cause of all these evils is the Archbishop of Narbonne, whose god is money, whose heart is in his treasury, who is concerned only with gold." Innocent tried to woo Raymond VI by lifting the excommunication the count had received in 1195 from Innocent's predecessor, Celestine III. Raymond seemed little interested, so Innocent tried the more direct tactic of writing letters that urged the count of Toulouse to do something about the Cathars. He did not mince his words. One letter rails at Raymond: "So think, stupid man, think!"

▼ When the Church's attention returned to the Cathar problem, much of the persecution was orchestrated by monks based at the abbey of Fontfroide.

Heresy Becomes Treason

Raymond was either unable or unwilling to persecute the Cathars, but Innocent had other means at his disposal. In April 1198, only two months after being made Pope, Innocent commissioned the Cistercians to preach in the Languedoc with the specific aim of bringing the heretics back into the fold of the Church. On March 25th, 1199, he issued the bull *Vergentis in senium*, which equated heresy with the Roman crime of treason against the Emperor, echoing the imperial statute *Lex quisquis* of A.D. 397. The punishment for heresy was to be the confiscation of property and the disinheritance

of descendants; the civil right of election and of holding civil office was also to be forfeited. If the heretics were clergy, they were to be stripped of benefices; if they were lawyers, they were to be forbidden to exercise office as judges. Although the bull was initially intended to cover Italy (specifically Viterbo, where the Cathar population was militant), Innocent planned to extend *Vergentis* to other lands as soon as circumstance allowed. The following year, Innocent suggested to the King of Hungary that he use *Vergentis* against heretics in Bosnia. Meanwhile in the Languedoc, papal legates arrived to begin the work of smoking out heretics and confiscating their property.

◀ Pope Innocent III is shown ex-communicating the Albigensians and calling for a crusade against all Cathar heretics.

An Enterprise of Peace and Faith

Innocent decided to replace his first legates—a certain John of St. Paul and his companion—with three new recruits in 1203. All of the men were southerners: Arnold Amaury was the Abbot of Cîteaux, while his two colleagues were both from the monastery of Fontfroide. Peter of Castelnau had been trained as a lawyer, and was violently disliked; he was subject to death threats while on his tour of duty in the South. The third Cistercian, Brother Ralph, seems to have been the least troublesome of the three, and had at times to use all his diplomatic skills to repair the damage caused by Peter. The legates were universally loathed, and were to play a crucial role in the events to come. Innocent referred to their undertaking as *negotium pacis et fidei*—the enterprise of peace and faith.

▼ Peter of Castelnau, a monk and papal legate, was charged with carrying out the destruction of the Cathar heresy.

The three legates' first tactic was to try to force the local nobility to swear oaths of allegiance to the Church and to agree to anti-Cathar legislation. Failure to do so would result in instant excommunication. Toulouse, Montpellier, Arles, and Carcassonne all agreed—at least in principle—with the measures the legates were proposing. Raymond VI was unhappy, however, because the anti-heretical statutes to which the consuls of Toulouse had agreed effectively diminished his rights as count. For the time being, he did what he had been doing all along when it came to persecuting the Cathars—nothing at all. The trio's second tactic was to invite the Cathars to debate with them, in public. Arnold, Peter, and Ralph hoped that they might be able to rouse the people as St. Bernard had done at Albi (rather than facing the humiliation the saint had endured at Verfeil). The first debate between 13 Cathars and 13 Catholics was held at Carcassonne in 1204, with Raymond VI's brother-in-law, King Peter II of Aragon, acting as the adjudicator. Both sides defined their positions eloquently, but the debate ended inconclusively. The papal legates were unable to have the Cathars put in chains or on pyres, and they left Carcassonne in frustration. It looked as though their efforts would be no more successful than St Bernard's at Verfeil after all.

After the Carcassonne debate, the situation became difficult for the legates. They were unpopular: The Cathars naturally regarded them as the servants of Satan, and the clergy were also uncomfortable with the presence of the three Cistercians, no doubt seeing them as a threat to their rich and cozy lifestyles. The nobility saw them as foreign meddlers, attempting to bring the ways of Rome to a land that had no need for them. Peter of Castelnau, angry at the response he had encountered, tendered his resignation in 1205, begging to be allowed to go back to Fontfroide. Innocent refused his request. (Although the Pope did not know it, he had just signed Peter's death warrant.)

And so the three men continued with their work, crisscrossing the Languedoc, haranguing nobles, and disputing with the Cathars. It was all to no avail; the heresy was too deeply entrenched. In Montpellier in the spring of 1206 the three Cistercians wearily concluded that they had failed. They were indeed in a land of many heresies, heresies

▲ St. Bernard of Clairvaux had successfully roused the people of Albi against the Cathars, but failed to do the same at Verfeil.

that had defeated St. Bernard and now had defeated—and would probably outlive—the three legates. However, at this point their luck began to turn. They were approached by two Spaniards, Diego de Azevedo, bishop of Osma, and his younger subprior, Dominic Guzman. Diego and Dominic told the Cistercians that they had seen the Perfect at first hand, and they had been impressed by the lives of simplicity, humility, and poverty that they led. The Perfect owned nothing except the clothes they stood up in and their holy books, a sharp contrast to the Cistercians, who traveled in pomp with a retinue of lackeys and bodyguards. The Spaniards suggested that Arnold, Peter, and Ralph beat the Cathars at their own game, citing the Biblical tale in which Christ sent out 70 messengers to the people ("Carry neither purse, nor scrip, nor shoes…"). The Cistercians were impressed, and agreed to the plan.

The Debate Runs its Course

That summer was a busy one. The legates, living in poverty according to the apostolic model, preached throughout the Languedoc. There were debates in Servian, Béziers, Carcassonne again, Pamiers, Fanjeaux, Montréal, and Verfeil. As with the first debate, these were lively and protracted affairs, sometimes lasting a week or more. Without the usual Roman regalia to hamper them, the papal legates were getting results: 150 Cathar Believers were said to have been converted after the Montréal debate. However, it was not enough. The enterprise of peace and faith had been in operation for three years, and the number of souls brought back to the Church was negligible considering the amount of effort expended. By the spring of 1207, the preaching and debating seemed to have run its course, and Arnold Amaury left to attend a Cistercian conference. Peter

▼ The great walls of the fortified city of Carcassonne are an enduring symbol of Cathar resistance.

▲ The castle at St Gilles, which was the power base of Raymond VI in the Languedoc.

of Castelnau was less easily discouraged, and spent the rest of the year trying to get various Languedocian nobles to start rounding up the Cathars. Ralph followed in his wake, trying to keep Peter away from the crowds, almost all of whom detested him heartily. In the debates that remained, Fulk of Marseilles took his place. Dominic continued to preach, and managed to found a convent for former Cathar women at Prouille.

Raymond VI again proved to be an obstacle to the mission. Peter visited the count of Toulouse at a time when he was conducting one of his wars, this latest one being against his vassals in Provence. Peter asked Raymond to turn his attention away from conducting private wars using mercenaries and to begin to actively pursue the heretics. Raymond protested that he couldn't do without his mercenaries because they were a vital component of his power base. He refused to swear an oath of allegiance, and Peter excommunicated him on the spot. It was Raymond's second excommunication, but it would not be his last. Peter's final words on the subject echoed around the hall in which he and Raymond— and numerous other nobles—were gathered: "He who dispossesses you will be accounted virtuous; he who strikes you dead will earn a blessing."

Raymond now took a conciliatory stance. He agreed to begin deploying his soldiers against the Cathars, and by the summer his excommunication had been lifted. In the autumn it became clear that he was doing nothing, and he was excommunicated again. By now, all parties were becoming exasperated with the situation. Pope Innocent wanted action against the Cathars, while Raymond wanted the Catholic Church to stop meddling in his affairs. A new meeting was arranged at Raymond's castle at St Gilles in early 1208. Exchanges between Raymond and Peter of Castelnau were heated. The recalcitrant count even threatened the papal legate with physical violence. On Sunday, January 13th, negotiations broke down completely. Peter left for Rome at first light next morning. He was never to get there. While Peter was waiting for the ferry across the Rhône, a hooded rider galloped up and put a sword through him. The identity of the assassin was never discovered, and it remains unknown. But it mattered little: The murder of Peter of Castelnau would have to be avenged.

▶ Peter of Castelnau, meeting his death at the hands of an unknown assassin on the way to Rome.

5 The Albigensian Crusade

CATHARISM SEEMED TO BE UNSTOPPABLE. THE THREATS
AND THE DIPLOMATIC EFFORTS OF THE CHURCH HAD FAILED
UTTERLY TO STEM THE TIDE OF HERESY. SO NOW THE POPE DID
SOMETHING COMPLETELY UNPRECEDENTED: HE CALLED FOR A
CRUSADE IN A CHRISTIAN LAND.

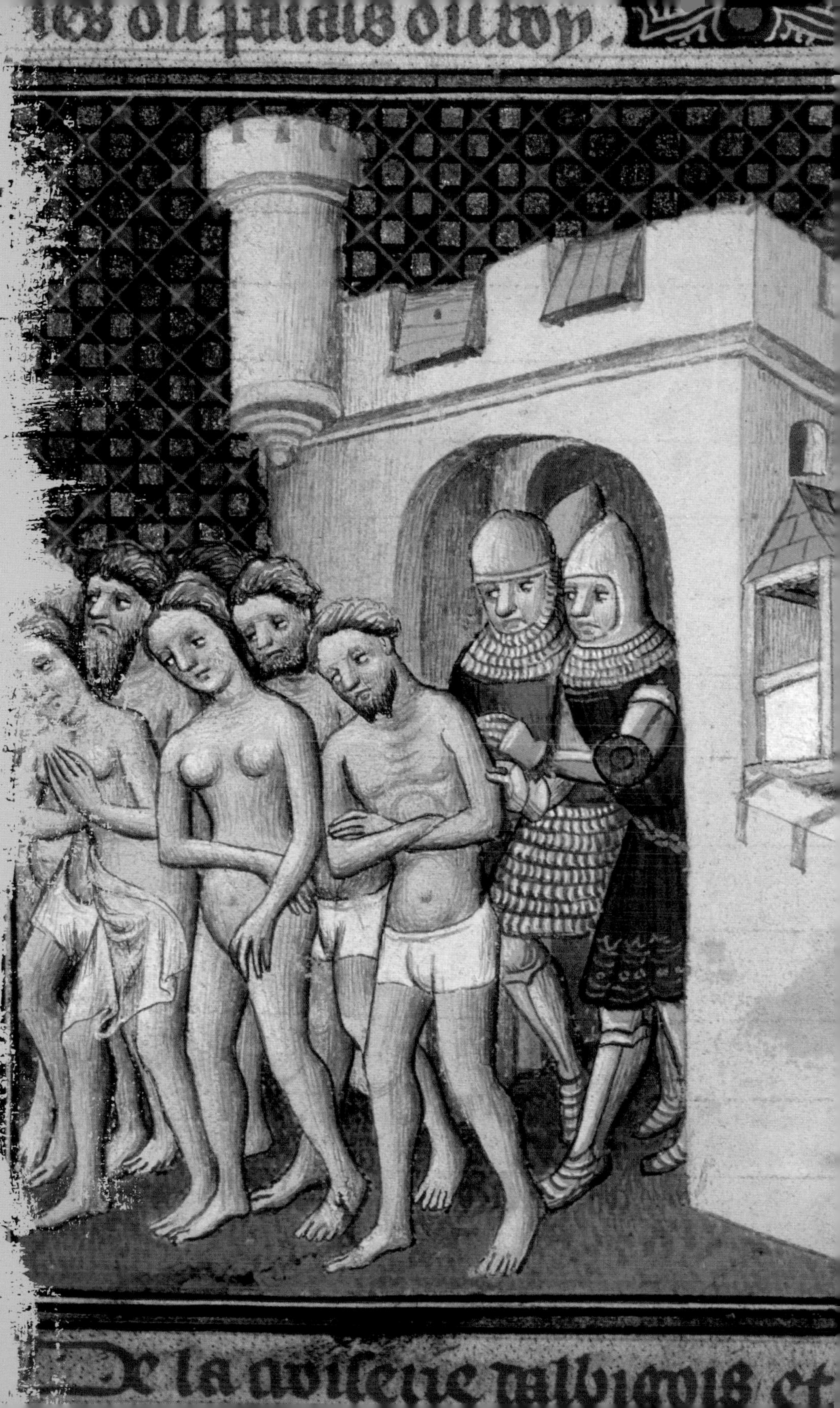
ies ou palais ou roy.
De la

Introduction

When Innocent heard the news of Peter's murder, he is said to have buried his face in his hands, then gone to St. Peter's to pray. Raymond VI expressed no apology for Peter's death, and though it could not be proved that he had ordered the murder, his lack of sorrow looked like an admission of guilt. This was a huge diplomatic error on Raymond's part. It did not matter that Peter had many other enemies in the Languedoc. Innocent was convinced of Raymond's complicity in the killing.

On March 10th, Innocent called for a Crusade. He had been considering a campaign in the South since the previous November at least. The Crusade was to be preached by Arnold Amaury and Fulk of Marseilles, who spent the better part of 1208 rallying support from kings and nobles across Europe. Many were too busy fighting each other to do the Pope's bidding, but Arnold's and Fulk's persistence paid off, and, by the middle of the following year, a ragtag army of nobles, knights, and mercenaries was on its way. Innocent had given the men the full Crusade indulgence: Forgiveness of all sins, cancellation of debts, and the promise of booty in the shape of land confiscated from the Cathars and their sympathizers. As was feudal custom, Crusaders had to serve for only 40 days before being released from their military obligations. The Languedoc also had the advantage of being easier to get to than the Middle East. Crusaders flooded down the Rhône valley.

Innocent had not given up entirely on diplomacy, but the deaths of Ralph of Fontfroide and Diego of Osma within 18 months of Peter's assassination had left the Church without two of its most valuable diplomatic assets in the South. Raymond had not given up on his own brand of diplomacy either. After failing to persuade Raymond Roger Trencavel, the 24-year-old viscount of Carcassonne, Béziers, and Albi to join him in submitting to the Church—possibly as an attempt to keep the Crusaders off his lands—the count of Toulouse agreed to undergo a humiliating penitential scourging at the church of St. Gilles. He was stripped naked and

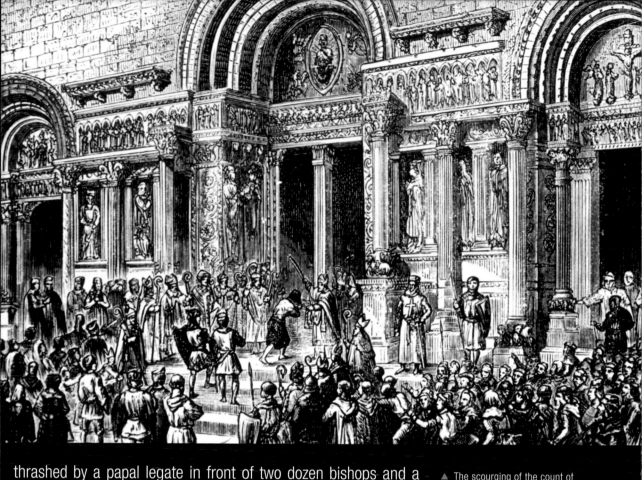

thrashed by a papal legate in front of two dozen bishops and a huge crowd of Toulousains, before being led into the church to swear allegiance to both the Church and the Crusade. He agreed to serve for the required 40-day period, but the demands forced on him did not stop there: He also had to renounce any claims he might have over religious institutions on his lands, and to apologize to all the clergy he had insulted, extorted money from, and harassed. Seven of his castles had to be forfeited, and he was banned from using mercenaries. All the Jews he employed had to be dismissed. In respect of the Cathars, he was to do as he was told: It was up to the Church, not the count of Toulouse, to decide who was a heretic and who wasn't. If Raymond reneged on the agreement, he was to be judged by papal legates. It was harsh treatment, and everyone knew it. The count of Toulouse had been made an example of. It was June 18th, 1209, and apocalypse was only weeks away.

◄ Previous page: The Cathar stronghold of Cordes-sur-Ciel in Languedoc was founded by Raymond VII.

The Crusade Begins

 Raymond Roger Trencavel knew time was running out, but was confident that, as a Catholic, he would be able to parley with the Church. After all, most of Innocent's efforts had been directed against Raymond VI, the Cathars, and Cathar supporters who lived on his lands, and he must have thought that he was in

a strong position. He was wrong. The Trencavels had a record of antagonizing the Church. In one of his boldest moves, Raymond Roger had kicked out the bishop of Carcassonne and installed his own man. The new bishop's mother, sister and three of his brothers were Cathar Perfect. Realizing that Raymond VI had played a canny hand by undergoing his scourging and submission, Raymond Roger also offered to submit to the Church, join the Crusade, and take action against the Cathars. Arnold Amaury refused his help. The crusading army moved toward Béziers, while Raymond Roger retreated to Carcassonne.

Béziers—which had refused to hand over its Cathars to the Cistercians in 1205—was annihilated on July 22nd. Such was the scale of atrocity that even Crusade apologists such as Peter of Les Vaux-de-Cernay felt the need to distance themselves from it by blaming the bloodbath on the *ribauds*, the mercenaries. Even by medieval standards, the events at Béziers were brutal. Nevertheless, there were some in the Church who felt that the slaughter was justified. Arnold certainly thought so, and wrote to Pope Innocent that "the workings of divine vengeance have been wondrous."

News of the atrocity at Béziers spread quickly. The Crusaders marched on Narbonne, which, fearing a similar fate, surrendered at the first sight of the papal army. Raymond Roger Trencavel knew that Carcassonne would be the next target. He implemented a scorched-earth policy around the city to make the land as inhospitable as possible for the Crusaders, who arrived on August 1st. The following day, the suburb of Bourg, which lay outside the city walls, fell. Further progress was halted by the arrival of King Peter II of Aragon. He came asking to speak to Raymond Roger, who was his vassal. Peter informed Raymond Roger that he had brought the Crusade on himself by allowing Cathars—"a few fools and their folly," as he described them—to live unmolested in his

◄ A knight leads the Albigensian Crusaders into Béziers, where they would lay waste to the city, and kill all of the inhabitants.

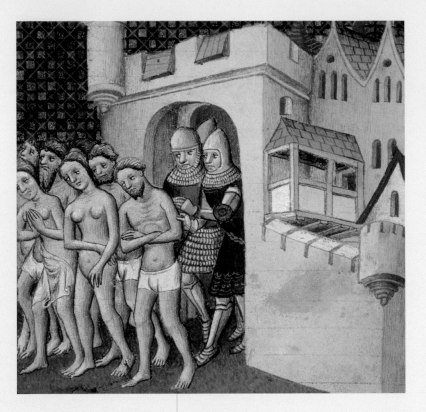

▲ Cathars were expelled from Carcassonne after the city was captured by Crusaders.

city. Peter urged negotiations, since the size of the crusading army vastly outnumbered Raymond Roger's men. Talks began, and Arnold Amaury guaranteed Raymond Roger safe passage from the city once the surrender had been effected; the fate of the city's inhabitants would be left to the discretion of the Crusaders. Peter was disgusted at the terms offered and went back to Aragon without having brokered an agreement. So the siege dragged on. With the fall of Bourg and its wells, Carcassonne had lost its supplies of fresh water. It was not long before the city was riddled with typhoid and dysentery. Raymond Roger was coaxed out of the city to discuss terms of surrender. The precise details of the deal are not known, but Raymond Roger negotiated to save the lives of all the people of Carcassonne—including all the Cathars—on condition that they leave the city. On August 15th, they did just that. They were not allowed to take with them anything more than the clothes they were wearing; many emerged from the gates barefoot. Arnold reneged on the promise he had made to Peter of Aragon, and had Raymond Roger clapped in chains in the dungeon of his own castle. He died there on November 10th, allegedly of dysentery. By then, Raymond Roger's lands, and the leadership of the Crusade, had passed to an obscure noble whose name was to become associated with ruthlessness and terror on a scale never before seen: Simon de Montfort.

Simon de Montfort

Simon de Montfort came from a family of middling wealth. The de Montforts owned lands in the North, near Paris, and also possessed the earldom of Leicester, with which Simon's fourth son, another Simon, would become closely associated. Simon was a fearless warrior—almost suicidally so at times—but he was also a man of principle. During the Fourth Crusade, he had refused to take part in the sack of the port of Zara on the Adriatic because the Crusade was meant to be attacking Muslims, not fellow Christians. He left that Crusade disillusioned. In the Albigensian Crusade, Simon at first played only a minor part, but he distinguished himself during an attack on the Carcassonne suburb of Castellar.

After the fall of Carcassonne, Arnold Amaury began to look for a successor to Raymond Roger. He approached the nobles one by one, but all declined for political reasons, fearing a jealous reaction from Philip Augustus, the King of France. Simon, with his modest holdings in the North, was deemed a safe choice, especially since his military credentials and piety were beyond reproach. So the Trencavel lands had a new viscount, and the Albigensian Crusade a new leader.

Simon first task was to deal with the tricky military situation. Winter was drawing on, and most of the northern nobles had returned home. A number of castles that

▼ Simon de Montfort, under whose generalship the Cathars were ruthlessly punished during the Albigensian Crusade.

had submitted to the Crusaders in the wake of Béziers had been retaken by southern forces. Indeed, resistance to the northerners was to be a near-permanent feature of the Albigensian Crusade. At Lombers there was even an attempt on Simon's life. No doubt such actions reinforced Simon's belief that he was fighting a just war. The towns of the Languedoc were not seen as Christian, like Zara: They were heretical and so by definition unchristian. The only way to bring them to submission was through merciless brutality.

The campaign season of 1210 got off to just such a start. In early April, Simon had taken the small town of Bram after a siege lasting just three days. He ordered 100 of Bram's defenders on a forced march. Before being sent on their way, the men were blinded, and had their noses and upper lips cut off. The man at the head of the procession was left with one eye, so that he could guide his mutilated

◀ Inhabitants await their fate during the siege of Carcassonne at the hands of the Crusaders.

▼ In spite of its location and high walls, still evident today, Carcassonne was eventually to fall to the crusading army.

comrades to Cabaret, a town 20 miles or so (about 30 kilometers) distant, which was known to be sheltering Cathars. It was a hideous warning, and Cabaret itself would fall to Simon within the year.

In June, the Crusaders besieged Minerve, a town perched on rocky cliffs 30 miles (45 kilometers) to the east of Cabaret. A huge trebuchet nicknamed The Bad Neighbor began bombarding the stone staircase that led to the town's wells, which lay at the foot of the cliffs. Once the wells were inaccessible, all the Crusaders would need to do was wait; like Carcassonne, the town would have to submit. Despite an attempt by Minerve's defenders to set The Bad Neighbor alight, the trebuchet continued to bombard the town in July. With the water supply cut off, Minerve's lord, William, had no option other than to surrender. He offered Simon all of his lands and castles on the condition that everyone within the walls of Minerve be spared. Simon agreed. He was just about to let the exhausted defenders of Minerve leave when the papal legate, Arnold Amaury, arrived.

Arnold, superior in authority to Simon, told William that everyone could go free on condition that they swore allegiance to the Church. All the townspeople did so. However, swearing oaths was anathema to the Cathars, and swearing one of allegiance to Rome unthinkable. Just three of the Cathars went back to Catholicism, but the rest remained unrepentant. On July 22nd, 1210, exactly a year to the day since the atrocities at Béziers, all 140 Cathar Perfect in Minerve were burned in the valley below the town. It was the first mass burning of the Crusade. It would not be the last.

▼ When the 140 Cathars among the townsfolk of Minerve refused to swear allegiance to Rome, they were burned alive on the instructions of the papal legate Arnold Amaury.

The Trencavel Towns Fall

After Minerve, the remaining Trencavel *castra*—fortified towns—of Montréal, Termes, and Puylaurens fell to Simon's forces. It was while besieging Lavaur in the spring of 1211 that Simon's tactics reached new extremes of cruelty. He was no doubt enraged by the fact that reinforcements from Germany had been wiped out by Raymond Roger of Foix at Montgey near St Félix the day before they were expected to arrive at Lavaur. Simon's forces breached the walls of Lavaur on May 3rd. With flagrant disregard for the conventions of medieval warfare, all 80 knights defending Lavaur were hanged, as was its lord, Aimery of Montréal, who was suspected of being a Cathar Believer. His sister, Geralda, was famed for her generosity toward Cathars who had been displaced from towns that the Crusaders had already taken. She was thrown down a well and stoned to death. All the town's Perfect—around 400 people—were burned at the stake. It was the largest mass execution of the Crusade. Later in the same month, between 50 and 100 Perfect were burned to death outside the town of Les Cassès. If one were looking for proof that the world was as evil as the Cathars believed, one need to look no further than the events of May 1211.

Toulouse was the next town in Simon's sights. The siege started the month after the bonfires at Lavaur. Within the town walls, Raymond VI had been having a difficult time. He had been excommunicated yet again in September 1209 for failing to show enough commitment to the Crusade. The count had then journeyed to Rome to bargain with Innocent, who allowed him to remain within the Christian fold, but only just. He then began a frantic diplomatic campaign, making good on all the promises to which he had committed during his scourging the previous June. Toulouse, meanwhile, was being terrorized by its bishop, Fulk of Marseilles. He had organized a vigilante group called the White Brotherhood, whose main activity consisted of nightly attacks on the homes of Cathars and Jews. In response, the

▶ Under the terms of a document issued by Simon de Montfort, lands belonging to Raymond VI were transferred to Philip II of France.

✠ IN : NOIE : SCE : ET : INDIVIDUE : TRINITATIS : AMEN : PH

dei gra franc Rex. Nouerint uniuersi psentes parit z futur. qd nos dilcm z fidele nrm
Simj Comite de Monte Forti recepim' in hominem nrm ligium de Ducatu Narbones.
Comitatu Tholosano. uicecomitatu Bitterren z Karasson. de feodis salicet z tris que
Raymund' qndam Comes Tholosan' de nobis tenebat que acqsita sunt sup hereticos et
inimicos ecce xpi salvo iure alieno z illox qui sunt homines nri dm tamen ad heam
fider xpiane. Vt ut ppetue stabilitatis robur obtineat. psentem carta sigilli nri auctori
tate z regij nois karactere inferius annotato roboramus. Actm ap Pontem Archie
Anno dnice Incarnationis. qO CC sexto decimo. et regni uo nri Anno Tricesimo septimo.
Astantibz in palacio nro quox noia supposita sunt z signa. Dapifero nullo Signum
Guidon buticular Signum Barth Camerar Signum Drech Constabular

DATA VACANTE PH S L CANCELLARIA

An illustrated manuscript showing the battle of Muret at which Simon de Montfort defeated the forces of Raymond of Toulouse and Peter II of Aragon.

Toulousains formed the Black Brotherhood, who clashed with the Whites on the city's streets on an almost daily basis. Raymond was excommunicated for a fifth time at the Council of Montpellier in February 1211 after refusing to obey its directives; the price of remaining in the Church would have been all his possessions and titles. When Simon called off the siege of Toulouse after only two weeks, it was a rare lull in the hostilities.

Peter II of Aragon was troubled by the threat posed to Toulouse and Raymond's lands. He attempted to negotiate with Innocent. He knew he was in a strong position: He had been one of the commanders of the crusading army that had achieved a decisive victory over Moorish forces on July 16th, 1212 at the Battle of Las Navas de Tolosa in Andalusia, and so was seen one of the heroes of Christendom. He argued that the Crusade had betrayed its original purpose—that of exterminating the Cathars—because it was now becoming evident that Simon de Montfort had killed at least as many Catholics as Cathars, and was engaged in building a fiefdom for himself. Peter proposed that he should be appointed guardian of all of Raymond's possessions, which would then pass to the count's son, the future Raymond VII, when he came of age. As part of the deal, Peter undertook to eliminate any vestiges of Catharism.

Innocent weighed up Peter's proposition, and was prepared to do as the Aragonese king suggested. On January 17th, 1213, he stunned Church forces in the Languedoc by announcing the end of the Albigensian Crusade, and instructing Simon de Montfort to return lands to the counts of Foix, Comminges, and Béarn. Arnold Amaury protested loudly, arguing that the Crusade still had work to do since the Cathars remained very much at large. The remaining southern nobles—the counts of Toulouse, Foix, and Comminges among them—agreed to Peter's plan to let him rule over all of the Languedoc. However, on May 21st, Innocent was finally swayed by Arnold Amaury, and reinstated the Crusade.

Simon de Montfort swung back into action, but, on September 12th, found himself confronted by a huge army of southerners led by Peter outside the town of Muret. Although greatly outnumbered, the Crusaders routed the southern and Aragonese forces. Peter himself was killed. The battle was a disaster for the South, with at least 7,000 men being killed. It was Simon's greatest victory. He was now effectively lord of all the Languedoc.

◄ The battle of Muret in 1213 was a particularly bloody episode in the Albigensian Crusade. More than 7,000 people were killed.

6 The Battle Continues

THE ALBIGENSIAN CRUSADE WAS ONE OF THE BLOODIEST EPISODES IN EUROPEAN HISTORY. HOWEVER, DESPITE THE SYSTEMATIC PERSECUTION, CATHARISM CONTINUED TO HOLD SWAY IN VAST TRACTS OF SOUTH-WEST FRANCE AND ITALY.

The Fourth Lateran Council, convened in November 1215, was the biggest gathering of churchmen for centuries. Of the preceding councils—held in 1123, 1139, and 1179—only the last had any business with heresy; then it had been deemed acceptable to use force against heretics. By the time of the Fourth Lateran Council, that force had been a reality for six long and bloody years. All of the major figures of the Albigensian Crusade, with the exception of Simon de Montfort and representatives of the Perfect, were in Rome. Even Raymond VI, that veteran of excommunication, was present, as was the fearsome Raymond Roger of Foix. The southerners had business with Innocent, and they were determined to be heard.

After a month of dealing with other issues—including the preparations for the Fifth Crusade, and the decision to force all Jews and Muslims to wear a yellow mark on their clothes to distinguish them from Christians—Innocent finally found the time to address the situation in the Languedoc. It was as grave as ever. At the start of proceedings, Fulk of Marseilles, bishop of Toulouse, angrily lambasted Raymond Roger of Foix for his toleration of Cathars on his lands, and for his role in the massacre of Crusaders at the village of Montgey. Raymond Roger retaliated

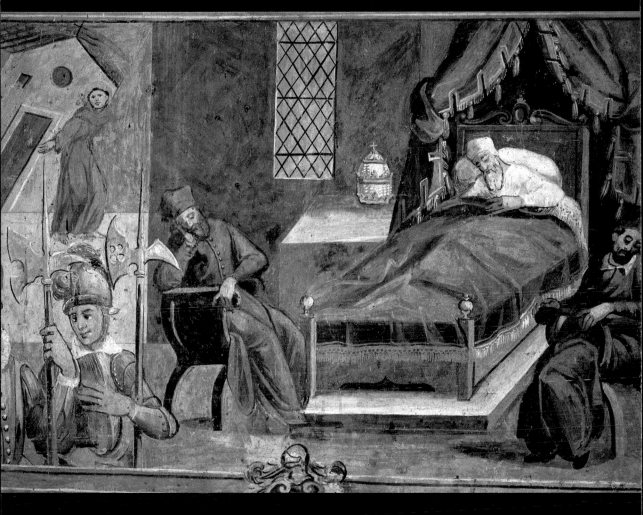

by hurling abuse at Fulk, saying that he was only sorry he hadn't killed more Crusaders. The poisonous atmosphere caused Innocent to go out into the gardens of the Lateran Palace to try to regain a clear head. By the time he came back in, he had decided to allow

▲ Pope Innocent's allegorical dream, in which he had a vision of St. Francis supporting the walls of the Lateran basilica.

Simon de Montfort to retain all his lands in the Languedoc. Raymond VI's son, Raymond the Younger, would become heir to various smaller possessions, but Simon would now officially be the count of Toulouse. It seemed to be the final nail in the coffin for the Languedoc.

The Siege of Toulouse

When news of the Pope's decision was heard in Toulouse, there was uproar; de Montfort would be denied access to the city. He was, after all, universally hated. Resistance was strengthened by the unexpected military victory of Raymond the Younger, who took the Crusader-held town of Beaucaire. Then Innocent died unexpectedly on July 16th, 1216. It seemed as though events might be moving in favor of the South.

Simon de Montfort's reaction to the revolt in Toulouse was swift and brutal. He was aided by Fulk of Toulouse, who persuaded the city's dignitaries to discuss terms outside the city walls. Either Fulk was remarkably convincing, or the city fathers remarkably forgetful of what had happened to Raymond Roger Trencavel at Carcassonne,

▶ A relief from the sarcophagus of Simon de Montfort depicting the successful siege of Toulouse.

but they took the bait. They left the safety of the city, and were put in chains as soon as they reached Simon's camp. With no one left to coordinate its defenses, Toulouse fell almost immediately to the Crusaders, who spent a month sacking the city. Simon then imposed exorbitant taxes on the beleaguered Toulousains.

Simon then made a fatal mistake. Despite the fact that Arnold Amaury had recently excommunicated him for his bullying tactics in Narbonne, Simon continued to act as an agent of the Church and left Toulouse to harass the nobles of Provence. He left a garrison to hold the city, but the Toulousains immediately began to hoard weapons and devised plans to revolt against this most hated of men. On September 13th, 1217, Raymond VI reentered the city under the cover of a dawn mist; the populace was ecstatic. Despite the fact that Raymond was an almost notoriously bad military commander—at the battle of Muret he had famously done nothing—the Toulousains felt that salvation was at hand. Raymond immediately ordered the rebuilding of the city's defenses. Simon's garrison was annihilated.

When he heard the news, Simon rushed back to Toulouse, intent on atrocity. Much to his surprise, he was thwarted time and time again. Despite the arrival of reinforcements from the North, Simon's forces could not breach the city walls. The stalemate lasted nine months, until June 1218, when the Crusaders decided, somewhat belatedly, to use siege engines to breach the walls of Toulouse. On June 25th, while fighting alongside his siege engineers, Simon de Montfort was killed, his head destroyed by a stone launched from a catapult on the walls of Toulouse. According to tradition, the catapult was operated by women and girls. The most hated man in the Languedoc was dead; no revenge was ever sweeter.

The seal of Raymond the Younger who was to become Raymond VII.

The Dawn of a New Order

Simon de Montfort's death marked the end of one of the darkest episodes in the history of western Europe. Most of the other protagonists in the Cathar drama died soon after him: Dominic Guzman died in 1221 (in 1234 he would be canonized as St. Dominic); Raymond VI in 1222; King Philip Augustus of France in 1223; Raymond Roger of Foix also died in 1223, and went to his grave still adamant that he should have killed more Crusaders; Arnold Amaury in 1225. In their place rose sons and heirs. Among them were men such as Raymond the Younger, who would become Raymond VII upon his father's death, and Roger Bernard, son of Raymond Roger of Foix. Both were able warriors, who had taken part in the defense of Toulouse in 1218 and in the subsequent southern resistance.

Simon de Montfort's son Amaury, on the other hand, was a less gifted soldier than his father. After Simon's death, he spent six years in constant conflict with Raymond the Younger and Roger Bernard. In the course of this debilitating standoff the de Montfort lands began to crumble away. In 1221 Amaury tried to found a military religious order dedicated to fighting heresy and modeled on the Knights Templar, but nothing came of it. Amaury's incompetence undid virtually everything that his father had achieved.

Innocent had long wanted the French crown to intervene in the South, but it was not until 1215 that Louis, son of Philip Augustus, launched an expedition of his own. It failed. In 1219, Louis tried again, committing a wholesale slaughter at the small market town

▲ Dominic Guzman, who died in 1221 and was canonized as St. Dominic in 1224.

of Marmande, where all 7,000 inhabitants were killed. He then attempted to take Toulouse, but failed and went back to Paris. The Albigensian Crusade further withered under Innocent's successor, Honorius III (1216–1227). He had another Crusade to deal with, the official Fifth, which began in the first year of his pontificate. While he saw the need to continue the fight against heresy, he did not put all his faith in crusading. He also saw the value of preaching, and gave his blessing to Dominic Guzman's Order of Preachers (better known as the Dominicans) and to the Franciscans. Both orders were to grow exponentially in the following years, and both Dominic and Francis were later canonized.

The Perfect began to reemerge during this period. Those who had survived Simon de Montfort had done so by hiding in caves, or in the Pyrenean fortresses of Montségur and Quéribus. In 1223, the Cathar bishop of Carcassonne, Peter Isarn, had copies made of the records of the meeting at St Félix so that he could determine and reestablish his diocesan boundaries after the havoc wrought by the Albigensian Crusade. In 1226, there was another major Cathar gathering at Pieusse. It was not as epoch-making as St Félix, but the fact that it happened at all showed that the Cathar church was far from beaten, and was confident enough to resume something approaching normal life; the council even established a new bishopric at Razès. But the peace was not to last.

It was Amaury de Montfort who inadvertently brought more grief to the Good Christians. After several years of losing ground to both Raymond VII and Roger Bernard of Foix, Amaury agreed a truce with Raymond in the summer of 1223. The following January, Raymond took control of Toulouse, and the following month Amaury admitted that he was beaten. He ceded all his claims to the Languedoc to King Louis VIII. The southern nobles now had a single powerful enemy: The French crown.

▶ St. Dominic oversees the burning of Cathar scriptures during the Albigensian Crusade, part of a policy to ensure that no trace of the written teachings would remain.

The Peace of Paris

King Louis was not the only person who wanted to settle matters in the South once and for all. The new papal legate to France and the Languedoc, Romano di San Angelo, was a ruthless and duplicitous man, the ideal person to continue harassing the beleaguered nobility of the South, and Raymond VII in particular. Raymond was operating under the supervision of the aged Arnold Amaury, who, since excommunicating Simon de Montfort, had—in the greatest irony of the whole saga—become sympathetic to the southern cause. Raymond and Arnold proposed a series of reparation payments to the de Montforts, in addition to Raymond swearing allegiance to the French crown and promising to drive the Cathars out of his lands. Romano, however, wanted the Crusade reinstated, and made sure that Raymond and Arnold's peace plan never came to fruition by excommunicating Raymond in early 1226.

▼ More than 3,000 Crusaders died during the siege of Avignon, but eventually the town capitulated.

▲ Avignon, with its famous bridge. The fall of this city proved to be a turning point in the campaign against the Cathars in France.

In the summer of that year, the Crusaders besieged Avignon. It was an uncomfortable standoff lasting three months, and Louis and his army succumbed to serious bouts of dysentery in the August heat. By the time the city finally surrendered, 3,000 Crusaders had died. However, word spread that the great city of Avignon had capitulated. From now on, the Crusaders would not have to do much fighting; their army was so huge that southern nobles offered their submission on first sight of it, or even on hearing that it was nearby. Under the threat of potential annihilation, former Cathar sympathizers such as Bernard Otto of Niort, the nephew of Aimery of Montréal and Geralda of Lavaur, suddenly became staunch supporters of the Crusade. The only real military challenges the Crusade faced were guerrilla attacks from the forces of Raymond VII and Roger Bernard

aler outre mer : de son tesins : ult chappee.

anice dessus ... cste amcur ce entente de
... mil et . lviii ... ... mcur : de ven see de finn
... le bon roy et ... ... adien : Adnert que la tir
lois qui toute sa bie auoit ... ... samte auoit besomg de

▲ An illustrated manuscript, the first half of which shows King Louis leading the Crusade; he is then seen on his deathbed after falling ill with dysentery.

of Foix, which proved a nuisance more than a real danger. Dysentery did more damage than the forces of Toulouse and Foix: Louis himself became seriously ill, and died on November 8th in Montpensier.

Louis's son, the future Louis IX, was only 12 at the time of his father's death, and his mother, Blanche of Castile, became Regent. She was determined that her husband's death would not be in vain, and pressed on with the campaign to subdue the southern nobles and eradicate Catharism. With Cardinal Romano as her principal adviser—they were even reputed to be lovers—she ordered her armies to remain in the South and to finish what her late husband had started.

In the late 1220s, the Crusade degenerated into a series of intermittent battles between Crusaders and the southern nobility. The situation might have carried on indefinitely, were it not for the fact that, in 1228, the Crusaders began to employ an extreme scorched-earth policy. This was much more thorough than the one Raymond Roger Trencavel had ordered at Carcassonne in 1209; this entailed the complete destruction of the countryside around Toulouse. Crops were burned, orchards felled, sources of water contaminated. The skies were black with smoke for a whole year. In 1229, with his lands an endless blasted heath, Raymond sued for peace.

On April 12th, 1229, history repeated itself. Raymond VII, like his father before him, was publicly flogged. The deal under which the flogging took place came to be known as the Peace of Paris, and the combined forces of Church and King had the count of Toulouse in a vice. Raymond's lands were seized by the French crown; he was left with little more than the city of Toulouse and a few minor towns, which he was allowed to retain for the rest of his life. He was also forced to marry off his only child, a nine-year old daughter, to one of the young Louis's brothers. In addition, Raymond was instructed to found— and fund—a new university in Toulouse, at which Church-approved doctors of theology would instruct new clerics in the Roman Catholic ways of righteousness.

▶ Next page: Quéribus Castle, one of the five so-called "sons of Carcassonne," was a stronghold of Cathar resistance in the 1250s.

▼ A depiction of the baptism of Louis IX, who came to the throne of France at the age of 12, on the death of his father.

Thus ended the Albigensian Crusade. Life gradually returned to normal in the Languedoc after 20 years of war, but St Bernard's original exhortation to catch the "little foxes" before they "ruined the vineyard" was now profoundly ironic: The vineyard of the Languedoc was indeed ruined, but the destruction had not been the work of the little foxes. And though they did not yet know it, the war-weary people of the Languedoc— Cathar and Catholic alike— had but little time to adjust to peace before they would face a new terror: The Inquisition.

7 The Inquisition

MILITARY INTERVENTION HAD CLEARLY FAILED TO ERADICATE THE THREAT POSED TO ROME BY THE CATHAR HERESY. SO THE ROMAN CATHOLIC CHURCH UNLEASHED A NEW FORCE THAT WAS AS SUBTLE AS IT WAS BRUTAL: THE INQUISITION.

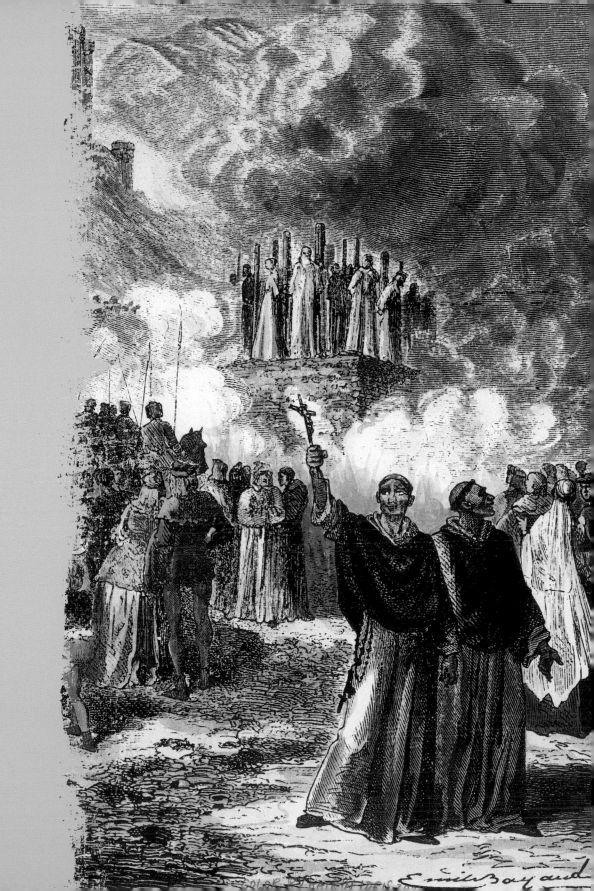

Introduction

While French troops reduced the Languedoc to a barren wasteland, devastation of another sort was being planned in the Lateran Palace. Pope Honorius had died in 1227. He was succeeded by Gregory IX, who was as much an activist Pope as his great forebears Gregory VII and Innocent III. Gregory—born Ugolino dei Conti di Segni—was one of Innocent's nephews and was as legally minded as his uncle had been. Gregory realized that if the Cathars were to be destroyed, then the Church needed the means to pursue individuals as much as the ability to intervene militarily. It was clear that the dualists were still active in the Languedoc and in other parts of Europe. The discovery of a Cathar community in Rome in 1231 can only have hardened Gregory's resolve.

The Inquisition was based on procedures drawn up under Innocent to tackle wayward priests. These rules granted the Inquisitors—usually Dominican friars—powers of arrest and trial. In the years that followed, a tool designed for keeping clergy in line became "one of the most effective means of thought control that Europe has ever known."

▶ St. Dominic presiding over the burning of heretics—an image designed to frighten people into remaining true to the Church.

◀ Pope Gregory IX, who with the help of the Dominican Order reinvigorated the campaign against the Cathars.

The Inquisition in the Languedoc

The Inquisition began its work in the Rhineland, but soon ran into difficulty. The chief inquisitor, Conrad Tors, was inclined to see heresy wherever he went. His indiscriminate arrests earned him many enemies, including the archbishops of Trier and Mainz, and in the end he was murdered by an enraged Franciscan friar.

Pope Gregory seems to have taken complaints against Tors seriously. He realized that if the Inquisition was to succeed, it needed to be far more methodical in its approach. Inquisitors were appointed in Toulouse, Albi, and Carcassonne in the spring of 1233. With their arrival in the south of France, the Inquisition proper came into existence. It was to remain a grim fixture of life in the Languedoc for the next hundred years.

▼ St. Francis of Assisi was known as a man of peace, but Franciscan monks were often pitiless in their pursuit of heretics.

When the Inquisition came to a town or a village, its officers would begin by talking to the clergy and briefing them on their procedure. The Inquisitors were then allowed to give a sermon in the church, in which they demanded a profession of faith from all males over the age of 14 and all females over 12. Those who did not or could not profess were automatically suspect, and would be the first to be questioned. The congregation was obliged to swear an oath against heresy and ordered to go to confession three times a year. The Inquisitors then asked those present to think about their past actions and prepare to make confidential statements the following week, either confessing their own sins or denouncing their neighbors. Cathars who voluntarily confessed were resettled in areas where no heresy was known, and made to wear two crosses sewn onto their clothes. Known or suspected heretics who had not confessed voluntarily within this first week were issued a summons to appear before the Inquisitors. Heresy, in the eyes of the Inquisition, included being a Perfect, sheltering one, "adoring" them (that is, performing the *melioramentum*), witnessing a "heretication" (that is, a *consolamentum*), and failing to report others. The Inquisitors needed at least two witnesses to convict a person. Witnesses' names were always withheld, which naturally made it easier for people to

119

accuse anyone against whom they bore a grudge. In a gruesome and deliberately shocking ploy, the Inquisitors did not limit the search for heretics to the living. If dead people were named as heretics, their bodies were dug up and burned. Any living relatives of the deceased had their homes and possessions confiscated, and they were forced to wear a yellow cross which was sewn to their clothes.

Once the Inquisition had its list of names, it was merciless in its pursuit of heretics. Inquisitors had the power to search a house, and to burn down any building where heretics were known to have hidden. Any person caught in possession of an Old or New Testament was seen as suspicious, and the sick and dying were watched closely lest "wicked and abominable things" occurred (that is, they received the *consolamentum*). Any heretic caught was subjected to a long and terrifying interrogation.

▶ At the Cistercian monastery in Moissac, monks were hiding Cathars, while at the same time, the Inquisition was burning others.

The ruthless fanaticism of the Inquisitors is graphically illustrated by the fate of a certain old woman in Toulouse. She was a Cathar Believer, and wanted to receive the *consolamentum* on her deathbed. Her family sent for a Perfect to come and administer the sacrament. A Perfect duly consoled the woman and left before the Inquisitors got wind of his presence. Somehow they got to hear of the deathbed *consolamentum*, and went to question the woman. Under the impression she was talking to a Cathar bishop, she talked about her faith. This was enough to condemn her. Though she had only hours to live, she was carried out of her house on her bed and burned.

Despite the power that they wielded, the agents of the Inquisition met with fierce and often violent resistance. In Albi, the Inquisitor Arnold Catalan's assistants were too frightened to enter the cemetery to dig up the body of a woman who had been posthumously accused

▶ Present-day Narbonne, where the Dominican monastery was sacked during a backlash against the persecution of Cathars.

of heresy. Incensed, Arnold went to the cemetery with several of the bishop's staff in tow. He broke the topsoil, intending to leave the hard digging to the bishop's underlings, but before any further work could be done, a mob set upon Arnold and beat him almost to death. It was only the timely arrival of an armed delegation from the bishop that saved the unconscious Inquisitor from being hurled into the River Tarn. While Arnold was recovering from his ordeal in the safety of the cathedral, a mob gathered outside, demanding that his head be cut off, put into a sack, and thrown into the river. In response, Arnold excommunicated the entire town. There were similar incidents elsewhere. At Cordes two agents of the Inquisition died when they were thrown down a well. In Moissac, Cistercian monks sheltered heretics while the Inquisitors burned others outside. In Narbonne, a Dominican monastery was sacked after an argument that flared up when a group of monks tried to arrest some heretics.

Raymond VII was initially supportive of the Inquisition—he was not in a position to be otherwise—but in 1235 there arose a chance to fight back. Relations between the Pope and Frederick II, the Holy Roman Emperor, were becoming increasingly strained. They had never been good: One of Gregory's first actions as pontiff had been to excommunicate Frederick for dallying over his crusading commitments. When Frederick did finally set off for the Sixth

Crusade in 1227, Gregory excommunicated him again for going on Crusade while his previous excommunication was still in force. Raymond offered to intervene in the Languedoc on Gregory's behalf on condition that the Inquisitors showed more restraint. Gregory agreed, and tried to curb the Inquisition's more fanatical agents in the Languedoc. Seeing that they had gained some ground, the Toulousains began to resist more strongly. Cathars and their sympathizers were hidden, or spirited out of town. In October, the Inquisitors were thrown out of Toulouse by a jeering mob, who pelted them with stones and excrement. Realizing he needed Raymond as an ally, the Pope could do little more than write the count an angry letter. He installed a Franciscan friar, Stephen of St. Thibéry, as the new Inquisitor, hoping that the Franciscans' reputation for being more humane than their Dominican brothers might go some way toward defusing tensions. Unfortunately, Stephen proved to be as fanatical as any Dominican.

▼ The seal of Raymond VII, count of Toulouse, who tried to curb the activities of the Inquisition in the Languedoc.

The Inquisition did achieve some successes. They gained inside information from two Perfect, Raymond Gros and William of Soler, who converted to Catholicism and provided the names of dozens of heretics. These two told the Inquisitors about the strategies that the Perfect had adopted to help them escape detection: Some male and female Perfect traveled in pairs, pretending to be married couples; some deliberately ate meat in public; others swapped their black robes for blue or dark green ones. Such ploys were seen as evidence of the cunning and deceit of heretics, though it was the tactics of the Inquisition that had made such cunning and deceit necessary.

The Trencavel and St Gilles Revolts

In the Languedoc, discontent grew as the Inquisition went about its detested business. Raymond Trencavel, son of Raymond Roger, attempted to capitalize on the ill will felt toward the agents of the Church. From exile in Aragon, he assembled an army that in 1240 besieged his ancestral seat of Carcassonne. After a tense and bloody standoff that lasted for more than a month, the two sides agreed a truce. Raymond Trencavel would never regain his birthright, but he had at least escaped with his life.

▼ King Henry III of England, who was persuaded to join forces with Raymond VII against the Pope.

Raymond VII had played no part in the Trencavel revolt, but on the death of Gregory VII the following year, he saw a chance to make a move. The papacy was in no position to stop him; Gregory's successor, Celestine IV, was Pope for only 17 days, and, due to Frederick II's attacks on Rome, it wasn't until June 1243 that his successor, Innocent IV, was elected. By the spring of 1242, Raymond had persuaded King Henry III of England and Hugh de Lusignan, the most powerful baron in Aquitaine, to join forces with him.

As if to announce the start of the revolt, the Inquisitors Stephen of St. Thibéry and William Arnold were murdered on May 28th at Avignonet by a small group of Cathar supporters from Montségur. News of the incident spread quickly, and was greeted with enthusiasm. One country priest even rang the bells of his church to celebrate the deaths of the inquisitors. Within days, Raymond's forces struck, taking French possessions and Dominican properties with decisive ease. By late summer it looked as if the coup would be successful, but then things began to go wrong. Henry landed with a force that was too small to be effective, and it was wiped out during an engagement with French forces near Bordeaux. Among Henry's knights was de Montfort the younger, whose change of sides was on a par with that of Arnold Amaury. Hugh of Lusignan, suddenly fearing he might be on the losing side, joined the French. The death knell of the rebellion, however, was sounded by none other than Roger Bernard of Foix. Despite his family's long history of pro-southern, pro-Cathar, anti-French activism, Roger Bernard, too, felt that the revolt was doomed, and negotiated a separate peace with the French. Raymond VII knew that all was lost, and he came to terms in January 1243. It was the end of his family's power in the Languedoc.

▶ Innocent IV, who became Pope in 1243. At that time, the Church was under attack in Languedoc. The leader of the uprising was Raymond VII, count of Toulouse.

The Fall of Montségur

One center of Catharism remained. This was the Pyrenean fortress of Montségur, the so-called "Synagogue of Satan." It had been a Cathar stronghold since the days of Innocent's "peace and faith" campaign. At a council at Béziers in 1243, it was decided that action had to be taken against Montségur. By the end of May, an army led by Hugh of Arcis, the royal seneschal in Carcassonne, was in place at the foot of Montségur. The fortress had a reputation for impregnability, so Hugh's army knew it was in for a long wait.

▲ The castle of Montségur had long been a refuge for Cathars. But in the end it fell to the Crusaders.

Montségur had been refortified in 1204 by Raymond of Pereille. He was a Believer, and both his mother and mother-in-law were Perfect. The castle had been a refuge for Cathars during the Albigensian Crusade. When the Inquisition began its work, Guilhabert de Castres, the Cathar bishop of Toulouse, approached Raymond with a request that the castle be made the center of the faith. By the time Guilhabert died (of natural causes) in about 1240, the castle was home to around 200 Perfect, who were overseen by Guilhabert's successor, Bertrand Marty. They were protected by a garrison of 98 knights, under Peter Roger of Mirepoix, whom Raymond of Pereille had appointed co-lord of Montségur at some point prior to 1240. Raymond had guessed—rightly—that the community would need armed protection as the Inquisition tightened its grip on the Languedoc. Peter Roger was from a family of Cathar Believers, but he had more in common with the bellicose Paulicians than the pacifist Perfect. He was happy to resort to armed robbery if that was what it took to keep the community fed, and he had been the instigator of the assassinations at Avignonet. In its heyday, Montségur had been a center of Cathar devotion and of industry. Pilgrims came great distances to hear the Perfect preach, to be consoled, or simply to spend time in retreat. When not busy with tending to the needs of the Believers, the Perfect helped support the community by working as weavers (a craft long associated with heresy), blacksmiths, chandlers, doctors, and herbalists. By the time the siege began, the total number of people living in Montségur—including the knights' families—was somewhere in the region of 400.

Hugh of Arcis did not have enough men to encircle the two-mile (three-kilometer) base of the mountain, and siege engines were useless in such craggy terrain. Hugh had no choice but to try to take the fortress by direct assault. His forces made numerous attempts to scale

▼ The rocky terrain at Montségur made it impossible to deploy siege engines. The fortress eventually succumbed to a nighttime attack.

the peak, but each time they were driven back by arrows and other missiles lobbed over Montségur's ramparts by Peter Roger's men. The months dragged wearily on, and by Christmas Hugh's army was becoming disillusioned. He needed a breakthrough to raise morale. He ordered an attack on the bastion that sat atop the Roc de la Tour, a needle of rock at the eastern end of the summit. The men climbed the Roc by night, and caught the garrison by surprise. The defenders were all killed. When daylight came, the royal troops looked down in horror at the sheer face they had scaled, swearing they could never have made the ascent by day. Their efforts gave the royal forces a strong foothold just a few hundred yards from the main castle. Work began immediately on winching up catapults and mangonels, and the bombardment of the citadel began.

▼ After Montségur was taken in 1244, more than 200 captured Cathars were burned at the stake.

Inside the walls of Montségur, the atmosphere of devotion intensified. While Peter Roger's men returned the French troops' fire, Bertrand Marty and Raymond Agulher, the Cathar bishop of the Razès, attended to the spiritual needs of both the garrison and the noncombatants. A messenger arrived to say that Raymond VII might intervene to liberate Montségur. There was also a rumor that Frederick II was planning a rescue mission. The weeks dragged on, but no one came. Finally, on March 2nd, 1244, Peter Roger walked out to announce the surrender of the fortress to Hugh of Arcis. The victors were lenient. They said that everyone could go free, provided that they submit to questioning by the Inquisitors and swear an oath of loyalty to the Church. Past crimes, including the assassinations at Avignonet, would be forgiven. The Perfect faced the same stark choice as their coreligionists at Minerve and Lavaur had done: Renounce Catharism or burn. They had two weeks to think about it.

For the Perfect, it was no choice at all. Not one of their 200-strong number was willing to recant. They spent the two weeks of the truce distributing their goods to their families and followers. Peter Roger was given 50 doublets that the Perfect had made, to sell or give away as he saw fit. On the final Sunday of the truce, 21 Believers—some of whom had originally gone to Montségur as mercenaries to help Peter Roger defend the castle, and all of whom had the option of going free—asked to be given the *consolamentum*. They knew that in doing so, they were giving themselves up to the pyres that were already being built at the foot of the mountain. If there is anything in the entire history of Catharism that illustrates the appeal and power of the faith, it is this extraordinary event.

▲ A memorial stone dedicated to the 200 Cathars who were martyred at Montségur.

At first light on Wednesday, March 16th, 1244, Montségur was evacuated. Peter Roger, his knights, and their families watched as the Perfect were lashed together on the pyres. They were from all walks of life and included Raymond of Pereille's wife and daughter. The 21 last-minute converts were there, as were Bertrand Marty and Raymond Agulher. Hugh of Arcis and Peter Amiel, the Archbishop of Narbonne, looked on as the pyres were lit. This place of execution is known to this day as "the Field of the Cremated."

The Inquisition after Montségur

With the last major redoubt of Catharism gone, Perfect and Believers found themselves in a world with little shelter and fewer protectors. No one was safe, as one Peter Garcias found out to his cost in Toulouse during Lent in 1247. His relative, William, a Franciscan, invited him to discuss issues of faith and doctrine. Peter had no qualms about telling William about his Cathar faith; after all, William was family. Peter railed against the Church of Rome, declaring that it was a "harlot who gives poison," while the law of Moses was "nothing but shadow and vanity." Peter was too trusting: A curtain was pulled back to reveal that his testimony had been carefully transcribed by a team of secretaries. Peter was handed over to the Inquisition.

William Garcias was not the only person to betray a family member to the Inquisitors. A former Cathar Perfect, Sicard of Lunel, denounced scores of his former associates and supporters "whether they had offered him a bed for the night or given him a jar of honey." The list of people he denounced included his parents. Sicard's treachery was amply rewarded by the Church, and he survived well into old age.

◀ The Inquisition was always careful to ensure that confessions were obtained before its victims were put to death, something that repressive regimes have continued to do ever since.

The Noose is Tightened

In the years after the fall of Montségur, the Languedoc was subject to inquisitorial scrutiny of Stalinist proportions. The two men heading this clampdown were Bernard of Caux and John of St. Pierre. More than 5,000 depositions survive from that time, but they are only a fraction of what was taken down. As Malcolm Lambert notes, Bernard, John, and their brethren were attempting to build "a total, all-embracing picture of Cathar belief, practices, and support in the areas in which they operated."

Capture presented a dilemma to any committed Cathars, since the Perfect were forbidden to lie or to swear oaths. Whatever they did, they would be compromising their beliefs. Some chose to tell the truth, and implicated other Perfect, Believers, and supporters, while

▼ The remains of the Cathar castle at Peyrepertuse. The fortifications are typical of the time.

◀ The castle of Puivert in the Languedoc which fell to Simon de Montfort in 1210.

others either lied or gave away as little information as possible. Yet others opted for collaboration and became double agents, continuing to live as Cathar Believers and receiving the fugitive Perfect into their homes, and then reporting them. Collaboration was risky, as there were frequent reprisals against turncoats. One such was Arnold Pradier, who had been a Perfect during the de Montfort years but later converted to Catholicism and began naming names. The Inquisition installed him and his wife in a safe house, the Château Narbonnais in Toulouse, where they lived well at the Church's expense.

Although resistance continued—at Castelbon, the Inquisitor was poisoned and the castle attacked—there was ultimately little people could do. The Inquisition became a fact of life, "an entrenched institution rather than a single, unrepeated ordeal." If people were suspected of giving false or incomplete testimony, they were hauled back in front of the Inquisitors to be interrogated again, regardless of whether they were a highborn noble or a peasant. Faced with such intensive action, most of the nobility realized there was no point in trying to oppose the Church; even Raymond VII began to persecute suspected heretics, burning 80 people at Agen in June 1249.

8 The Final Years

NEITHER WAR NOR PERSECUTION HAD MANAGED TO WIPE OUT THE HERESY OF CATHARISM ENTIRELY. IT LINGERED ON IN THE LANGUEDOC, AND CONTINUED TO FIND ADHERENTS IN OTHER CORNERS OF WESTERN EUROPE.

Introduction

Catharism became a ghostly presence. Despite the tireless efforts of the Inquisition, the deep roots that Catharism had put down had not been eradicated. Even after all the atrocities and hardships that the region had suffered over several decades, people still seemed unwilling to give up completely on the old religion. According to the testimony of Stéphanie de Châteauverdun, a noblewoman and Cathar Perfect from the Sabartès, any high-ranking Cathars that remained were living in the mountains. William Prunel was one such Perfect. His career stretched from around 1258 until 1283. It seems that he once spent a month in Toulouse, and was recognized as a Cathar, but no one betrayed him. William continued to spread the faith, and was known to have both nobility and clergy among his flock. Another Perfect, William Pagès, was also active during the same period; he had managed to survive by hiding out in Lombardy.

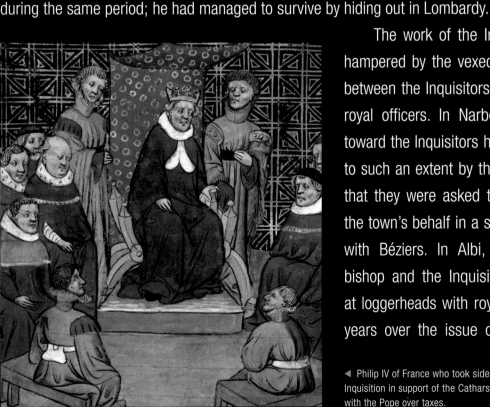

The work of the Inquisition was hampered by the vexed relationships between the Inquisitors, bishops, and royal officers. In Narbonne, hostility toward the Inquisitors had diminished to such an extent by the early 1260s that they were asked to arbitrate on the town's behalf in a secular dispute with Béziers. In Albi, however, the bishop and the Inquisitors remained at loggerheads with royal officials for years over the issue of confiscating

◀ Philip IV of France who took sides against the Inquisition in support of the Cathars following a dispute with the Pope over taxes.

the property of convicted Cathars: The bishop favored leniency to prevent families from being bankrupted, and was, remarkably, supported by the Inquisitors. Royal officials were attacked by crowds of locals. In retribution, the bishop's bastides—small

▲ By 1260 hostility to the men of the Inquisition diminished. In Narbonne, Inquisitors were even asked to arbitrate in a dispute with the town of Béziers.

fortified new towns—were pillaged by royal forces. The situation deteriorated further during the last two decades of the thirteenth century. Complaints against the Inquisitors became more frequent. In the 50 years before 1275, there were only two complaints, but between 1275 and 1306 there were 30. The Inquisition retaliated by accusing royal officials of complicity with heretics. Matters were further complicated by the relationship—not always harmonious—between the French king, Philip IV, and the papacy. Philip took sides against the Inquisitors. As a result of these tensions, arrests for heresy in the last years of the thirteenth century were largely political in nature. Once Pope Boniface VIII died in 1303, Philip withdrew his support and the Inquisitors got back to work relatively unhampered. As they did so, something quite unexpected happened: There was a Cathar revival.

Peter Autier

Peter Autier was from the small town of Ax-les-Thermes, up-country from Foix. He was born in around 1240, and had made a good life for himself as a notary. Peter had a wife, a mistress, and families with both women, a fact that did not harm his good social standing. During the 1270s, the family firm had done work for Roger Bernard III of Foix, and had gone on to win more state commissions, which had increased the firm's status and purse. Then in 1296, everything changed.

Peter and his brother William decided to go to Lombardy—where there were still active Cathar communities—to receive the *consolamentum*. There was a history of Catharism in Peter's family,

▶ Barolo in Lombardy, where Peter and William Autier found a strong Cathar community and where they were able to receive the *consolamentum*.

but it is still remarkable that Peter, knowing full well what he was letting himself in for, was prepared to turn his back on a very comfortable existence.

In early October 1296, he and William left for Lombardy. They traveled with Bon Guilhem, Peter's illegitimate son, and Peter de la Sclana, apparently a close associate. They were joined en route by one of Peter's daughters and her husband. Peter and William received the *consolamentum* from an Italian Perfect in Cuneo, a town in south-west Piedmont that had been a center for exiled Languedocian Cathars since the middle of the century. Then, around St. Martin's Day (November 11th) 1297, Bon Guilhem reappeared in Ax. He informed the Autiers' extensive network of family and supporters that Peter and William had become Perfect in Italy, and wanted to return as soon as it was safe for them to do so.

▲ Cathars were able to obtain food and sustenance from an extensive network of support across much of northern Italy.

Peter came back first, reaching Toulouse in the autumn of 1299. The purpose of his visit was to see a money changer, which suggests that securing the mission's finances was his priority. Despite careful planning, Peter's cover was blown almost immediately. He was recognized by Peter de Luzenac, the son of a rich widow whom Peter Autier had attempted to convert to Catharism three years earlier. De Luzenac was studying law at the time, and owed a great deal of money. Peter Autier bought his silence by paying off his debts.

Meanwhile, William reappeared in Tarascon, preparing the way for the missionary work to begin. While the brothers had been in Lombardy, they had kept in touch with family back home, and a wide network of safe houses had been established for the brothers to use on their return. During the winter and through into the spring of 1300, William and Peter Raymond of Saint-Papoul, another Perfect,

▼ Tarascon, where William Autier laid the foundations for his work as a missionary for the Cathar faith.

lived in a dovecote that belonged to a family of Cathars. Given the power of the Inquisition, Peter and William needed to act with stealth if their mission was to stand even the smallest chance of success.

Yet success is precisely what they achieved. The brothers recruited and consoled about a dozen others to help spread the word. Among their followers was Aude Bourrel, who was to

achieve the distinction of becoming the last known female Perfect. Bernard Marty—possibly a relative of the great Cathar bishop Bertrand Marty—was a shepherd who frequently acted as a scout and escort, while his older brother Arnold would become one of the Autier Perfect; Martin Francès from Limoux acted as the group's treasurer. This little network of Cathars received gifts from Bertrand of Taix, a minor noble and lifelong Cathar Believer who permitted these new converts to stay on his estates when need arose. Bertrand's wife was a devout Catholic, but she allowed her husband to support the Autier brothers, and did not betray him.

▲ The Autier group would receive gifts and financial support from local noblemen as well as a safe haven on their estates.

Almost as soon as the group began their work in the spring of 1300, they were in danger. They were approached by one William Dejean, who appeared to be a Cathar Believer. He expressed some interest in joining the Autier group, but the following day he visited the Dominican monastery in Pamiers, offering to betray the Cathars to the Inquisition. The friar he spoke to, Raymond de Rodes, was Peter Autier's nephew. De Rodes immediately told his brother William about Dejean's offer, and William then passed the news to Raymond Autier, the one brother who was not a Cathar. The pair realized that Dejean had to be dealt with at once. He was lured up a mountain pass, where four Believers beat him to a pulp. When questioned, Dejean was able to answer that he had been intending to betray the Autiers to the Inquisition. The four then threw Dejean over the cliff into the ravine below.

▶ The Autier Cathars lived like fugitives. By day they would often disguise themselves as tradesmen. At night they would sleep in sheds, barns, and cellars.

The *Endura*

Autier Catharism differed from that of earlier eras in that it had to operate clandestinely. There was no hierarchy: Peter Autier was not a bishop or a deacon, he was simply a Perfect, and that was enough. His Perfect traveled at night, guided by the likes of Bernard Marty over the mountainous terrain of the Sabartès. If they traveled by day, they disguised themselves as merchants or peddlers (Peter and William traveled back from their consoling in Lombardy posing as knife salesmen). They slept and taught in cellars, attics, dovecotes, sheds, and barns.

▼ The practice known as the *endura* required a newly consoled Cathar to refrain from taking any sustenance other than cold water.

The group's principal activity was administering the *consolamentum* to the dying. In a society deeply damaged by the Inquisition, where husbands concealed their Cathar beliefs from their wives and vice versa, the visits of the Perfect had to be discreet and expertly timed. Some of the consolings were audacious. A woman by the name of Gentille d'Ascou was dying in the hospital at Ax in September 1301. By the time William Autier arrived late one evening, she was too weak to walk or sit upright unsupported. As the hospital was also an unofficial brothel, William carried out the *consolamentum* in a field at the back of the hospital. In Tarascon three years later, he performed a *consolamentum* disguised as a woman.

Frequently, these *consolamentums* were followed by a practice called the *endura*. This required the newly consoled Cathar to refrain from taking anything except cold water while they lingered in this world. Fear of betrayal meant that the Perfect could not remain with the consoled to ensure that he or she did not deviate from the diet of a Perfect. The *endura* was a means of ensuring that the newly Perfected Cathar would remain true to the faith, and not sully the *consolamentum*. It meant avoiding sin by avoiding everything that might lead to sin. A woman named Gentille d'Ascou lasted for six days on cold water after her *consolamentum*. Another woman, Guillemette Faure, lying on her deathbed in December 1299, fasted in *endura* for a full 15 days.

Geoffrey d'Ablis and Bernard Gui

Things began to go wrong for the Autier group in 1305. James Autier and Prades Tavernier were lured into a trap by a man named Peyre in Limoux, and arrested. It could have spelled the end for the Autier network, but James and Prades managed to escape almost immediately. Nevertheless, the damage was done, and the Inquisitors discovered how widespread the Autier network had become—there were at least 1,000 Believers, scattered throughout 125 locations. However, the Autiers still had a great deal of support; Peyre's brother was murdered in Carcassonne in retaliation for his treachery, and Peyre was still in hiding under the protection of the Church as late as 1321.

A much greater challenge was to come. Around the time of the arrests, two men were appointed to run the Inquisition in the Languedoc: Geoffrey d'Ablis and Bernard Gui. They would go down in history as two of the most able churchmen ever to fulfil the role of Inquisitor. The confessions they extracted from suspects are so detailed that they are among the best records we have of Catharism. Perhaps the most notable example of the efficiency of the new Inquisitors occurred at Montaillou. On September 8th, 1308, the entire population of the village was arrested on suspicion of heresy.

The Last Perfect

With the renewed vigor inspired by d'Ablis and Gui, the Inquisition eventually caught up with nearly all of the Autier Perfect. They were arrested, interrogated, and burned during 1309–1310. Sans Mercadier, a young weaver who had been consoled in 1309, was not caught but committed suicide in despair. Peter Autier spent eight months in prison before being burned on April 9th, 1310 in Toulouse. Then in his late sixties, he remained defiant to the very end. As he was being tied to the stake, he asked to be allowed to preach to the crowd who had come to watch him die; Peter announced that he would convert all those present to Catharism. His request was denied, and, with his passing, there remained only one Perfect still at large in the Languedoc.

William Bélibaste was from the Corbières. Some time before Easter 1305, he had killed a fellow shepherd. Later that year, he met the Perfect Philip d'Aylarac who was traveling by night and wanted to take refuge in William's sheepfold. The meeting was to change Bélibaste's life. He joined the Autier network, and was consoled. In 1307, he and Philip d'Aylarac were imprisoned in Carcassonne on suspicion of being heretics, but they managed to escape in September of that year. Bélibaste seems then to have crossed over the border into Catalonia. After the Autier movement was destroyed by the arrests and burnings of 1309–1310, he remained in exile, where he tended to a group of Believers who had fled from the Languedoc.

Bélibaste's ministry was unusual. He kept a mistress, Raymonde Piquier, but outwardly kept up the pretence of celibacy required by the *consolamentum*. In 1319, he arranged for Raymonde to marry Peter Maury, a shepherd and Cathar Believer, in an attempt to fool people into thinking that Peter was the father of the child that Raymonde was carrying. Several days after the marriage, Raymonde and Peter were divorced and she moved back in with Bélibaste. Despite his dubious morality, Bélibaste was an inspired preacher

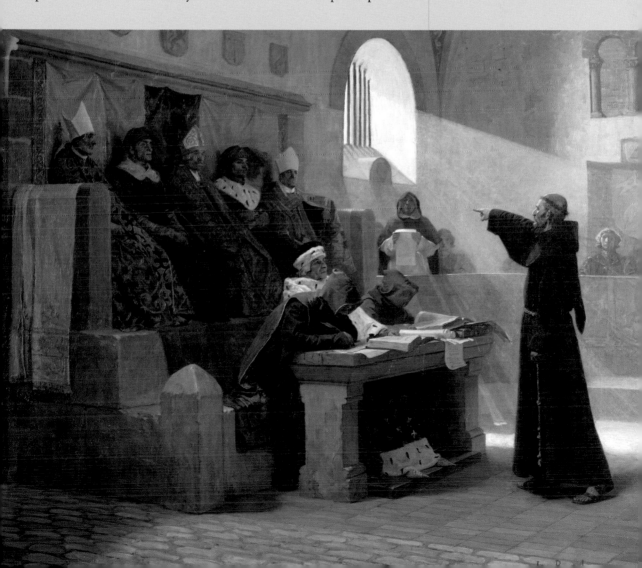

▼ Under the leadership of Geoffrey d'Ablis and Bernard Gui, the Inquisition became more effective and ruthless than ever.

who conscientiously guided his diminished flock as best he could. He urged his followers never to give in to despair, stressed the need to love one another, and praised the good God who was waiting for them all at the end of their earthly travails.

The group was troubled by the arrival of a newcomer, Arnold Sicre, in 1317. His credentials seemed respectable enough. He had come from Ax-les-Thermes, where his mother Sybille and his brother had

been burned by the Inquisition. He asked for instruction in the faith, but not all of Bélibaste's group were convinced he was genuine; his father was not a Cathar, and was known to have helped organize a raid on the village of Montaillou. Despite his dubious credentials, Sicre was admitted to the group, and found work locally as a cobbler. Within the year, Sicre informed Bélibaste that he wanted to search for his rich aunt and younger sister who lived, so he said, somewhere in the Pallars valley, a part of Aragon that bordered on the county of Foix. He made two trips north, each time returning with money that he said his aunt wanted Bélibaste to have. Finally, he announced that his sister, Raymonde, wanted to marry. Bélibaste decided that she would make a fine wife for Arnold Maury, Peter Maury's brother, who was one of the group. The prospect of a rich benefactress must surely have appealed.

Bélibaste set off with Sicre to meet the aunt and the sister around the middle of March 1321. It was a trick. Once they reached Tírvia, which was within Fuxian jurisdiction, Bélibaste was arrested. Sicre explained that he had betrayed him because he wanted to reclaim his mother's house, which had been forfeited when she had been burned. The aunt and sister had never existed; during his absences, Sicre had instead been visiting James Fournier, the bishop of Pamiers, who was spearheading a fresh wave of inquisitorial proceedings. Sicre's treachery did not stop there. Once Bélibaste had been put into custody, he immediately put himself into the *endura*, hoping to starve himself to death before he could be burned. Sicre convinced the Perfect that he was sorry for his actions, and told Bélibaste that he had devised an escape plan, which could be carried out only if Bélibaste were fit. So he abandoned his fast. Sicre had been lying again—there was no plan, no escape. Sicre had his mother's house restored to him, and continued to betray Cathars to the Inquisition. No record of Bélibaste's trial survives, but he was burned in the small town of Villerouge-Termenès.

◀ The continuing efforts of the Inquisition to wipe out the Cathar movement served to drive it even further underground.

9 No More Good Men

THE CATHARS WERE SUBJECTED TO MORE THAN A CENTURY OF UNREMITTING PERSECUTION. AT THE END OF THAT TIME, VIRTUALLY NO TRACE REMAINED OF A FAITH THAT HAD AT ONE POINT LOOKED SET TO TAKE POSSESSION OF EUROPE.

Introduction

Jacques Fournier, meanwhile, was interrogating afresh people who had been questioned ten years earlier by Geoffrey d'Ablis. Fournier was an even more thorough Inquisitor, and managed to extract a wealth of new information. In particular, he discovered that the situation in Montaillou was far more serious than had originally been thought. Almost everyone there had been, or still was, a Cathar. The information sparked a new wave of arrests. A number of factors had allowed Catharism to take hold of almost the entire village. There was no lord to oversee the villagers. He had died in 1299, and his widow, Béatrice de Planisolles, seems to have been converted—at least for a time—to Catharism by Peter Clergue, the village's rector. Although a Cathar, Clergue was still outwardly a Catholic priest, saying mass, hearing confessions, performing baptisms, and funerals. He was also notoriously promiscuous, bedding many of the women in the village, including Béatrice, with whom he once had sex in the church. Clergue's

▶ The castle close to Montaillou, where Jacques Fournier uncovered a thriving Cathar community.

◀ Jacques Fournier, bishop of Pamiers, whose efforts drove Catharism in Languedoc to the very brink of extinction.

brother Bernard was the village's bayle—an agent for the local count of Foix—and was also a Cathar. Together the two men controlled the life of the village, and so had the power to keep unwelcome visitors out.

Over the course of the 1320s Fournier sentenced hundreds of people. Béatrice de Planisolles was sent to prison. Her sentence was later commuted, but she still had to wear yellow crosses stitched onto her clothes—the traditional mark of the heretic. Various members of Bélibaste's group were jailed, including Peter Maury and his brother John, who were sentenced to "perpetual prison" on August 12th, 1324. Peter Clergue, the rector of Montaillou, died before he could be sentenced. On January 16th, 1329, he was pronounced a heretic, and his remains were dug up and burned.

This, at last, was the end of Catharism in the Languedoc. All the Believers who remained alive had been forced to confess and recant. There were to be no more consolings—and so ended a tradition which, the Cathars believed, had come down to them "from the time of the apostles until this time and it has passed from Good Men to Good Men until the present moment, and it will continue to do so until the end of the world." Now that there were no more Good Men, it seemed that the end of the world had indeed come to pass.

Thirteenth-Century Italian Catharism

At the start of the thirteenth century, Italian Catharism was a fractured church. Concorezzo and Desenzano were the bastions of the moderate and absolute schools of dualism respectively, while the *ordo* of other churches, such as those at Florence and the Val del Spoleto, remains unknown. As in the Languedoc, the political situation helped nurture the growth of Catharism. But unlike in the south of France, opposition did not generally come from Crusaders so much as from reforming movements that originated both inside and outside the Church. From within, the way was led by St. Francis of Assisi. He did not mention the Cathars—or Patarenes as they were frequently known in Italy—by name, but he stressed the importance of examining closely the beliefs of potential new recruits to the Franciscan Order. He wrote of the importance of regular attendance at both church and confession, and of the need to respect priests. He also stressed the physical reality of Christ's birth, which went against the Docetism of the Cathars.

There were also popular preachers who commanded the attention of huge crowds every time they gave a sermon. One of these was John of Vicenza, whose preaching led to the rise of the Alleluia movement, a popular, if shortlived, phenomenon in the tradition of the pro-reform Pataria of Gregory VII's day. John presided over the mass burning of 200 heretics—mainly Cathars and Waldensians—in Verona in August 1233. John's mission led to the founding of a number of lay confraternities, including that of St. Maria of Misericord in Bergamo, which were intended for people who wanted to further their spiritual practice without having to become monks or nuns. Their members swore to adhere to certain rules, such as refusing to shed blood or

► The court of Frederick II, Holy Roman Emperor, was a place where all manner of heretics and nonbelievers were tolerated.

bear weapons and refraining from an unethical way of life. They also actively worked toward the repression of heresy.

While these various movements served as outlets for people who were dissatisfied with traditional forms of religiosity, conflict between the papacy and the empire created circumstances in which Catharism could flourish. The reign of Emperor Frederick II (1220–1250) saw these confrontations reach a peak, and Italian politics came to be dominated by two factions, the pro-papal Guelphs, and the pro-imperial Ghibellines. Frederick did little to encourage the persecution of heretics, and the papacy, keen to gain allies in the key cities of Lombardy, did not press the heresy issue. Many cities did not enforce antiheresy legislation—not because their leaders were especially sympathetic to groups such as the Cathars or the Waldensians, but because any attempt to persecute heretics would have necessarily led to a greater role for the Church, thereby decreasing the cities' autonomy. Cathars were relatively free to go about their business under the protection of the Ghibelline nobility, and in Lombardy, a Languedocian Cathar church in exile flourished.

▶ Present-day Siena where Cathars were free to go about their daily business under the protection of a benign nobility.

The Decline of Italian Catharism

The pro-imperial Ghibelline party received a major setback with the death of Emperor Frederick II on December 13th, 1250. His son Conrad IV continued the struggle, but the papacy emerged victorious in 1268 with the capture and execution of Frederick's grandson Conradin, who was the last of the Hohenstaufen rulers. With the loss of their main ally, the Ghibellines went into decline, and the Cathars under their protection found themselves vulnerable to the attentions of the Inquisition. When the Inquisitor (and former Cathar) Peter of Verona was murdered by Cathar-hired assassins in 1252, Pope Innocent IV turned the event to the Church's advantage: Peter was canonized as St. Peter Martyr, and Innocent authorized the use of torture during inquisitorial procedure.

The intensification of the Inquisition's efforts drove many Cathars underground, or forced them to live double lives. One extraordinary case was that of Armanno Pungilupo of Ferrara. He was considered a pious Catholic and famed for his good works. After his death on January 10th, 1268, he was buried in the cathedral. His saintly reputation persisted, and miracles were reported around his tomb.

After much investigation by the Inquisition, it emerged that Armanno had been not just a Cathar Believer, but a Perfect for the last 20 years of his life. He had even survived a brush with the Inquisition in 1254, who tortured him, made him swear loyalty to the Catholic Church, and threatened to impose a heavy fine on him if he was caught engaging in heretical practices in the future. Armanno agreed, and carried on as before. One of the so-called miracles at his tomb, the case of a mute who suddenly regained the power of speech, was found to have been faked by a Cathar intent on lampooning the Church's cult of miracles. Armanno's remains were dug up and burned in 1301, and his ashes were thrown into the River Po.

By far the most serious loss the Italian Cathars sustained was the fall in 1276 of the castle at Sirmione, which stood on a peninsula extending into Lake Garda. Sirmione was the Italian Montségur. It had been home to various exiled Cathars, including the last known bishop of the northern French Cathar church, and the last Cathar

▼ ▶ Sirmione on Lake Garda in northern Italy. The suppression of the Cathar community here was a major blow to the movement.

bishop of Toulouse, Bernard Oliba. In February 1278, all 200 Sirmionese Perfect were burned in the amphitheatre at Verona.

Brute force and mass murder, however, were not the sole reasons for Catharism's decline in Italy. As Malcolm Lambert notes, "alternative paths to salvation had opened up." People were able to express their dissatisfaction with the Church in ways other than by becoming Cathars. Groups such as the lay confraternities played a large part in this, as did the enormous success of the Franciscans. Unlike in the Languedoc, where Catharism was consumed by a holocaust, Catharism in Italy faded away slowly. The last known Cathar bishop was arrested in 1321, and the last known Cathar in Florence was hauled up before the Inquisition in 1342. By this date, the only remaining Cathars were living in secretive communities in the Alps, where for several more decades they managed to elude the long arm of the Inquisition.

10 The Cathar Legacy

LITTLE WRITTEN TESTIMONY OF CATHARISM HAS SURVIVED, AND SO MANY QUESTIONS REMAIN—NOT ONLY ABOUT CATHAR THOUGHT AND PRACTICE, BUT ALSO ABOUT THE MOVEMENT'S RELATIONSHIP TO THE TROUBADOURS AND THE KNIGHTS TEMPLAR, AND TO THE MYTH OF THE HOLY GRAIL.

Introduction

Very few Cathar tracts have come down to us. Most of the surviving works come from Italy, where literacy levels were generally higher than in the Languedoc, and where the disputes between various Cathar factions encouraged polemicism. Moreover, Italy's geographical closeness to the Balkans meant that books arriving from the East, such as the Bogomil *Secret Supper* and *The Vision of Isaiah*, would generally first appear in the West on the Italian peninsula. These two works were known by the end of the twelfth century. *The Secret Supper* enlarges upon the Bogomil/Cathar creation myth, in which Satan is cast out of heaven for wishing to be greater than God. In this story, Satan pretended to repent, so God forgave him and let him do what he wanted. With his newfound freedom, Satan created the world of matter, and made human beings from the primordial clay. Each soul was a trapped angel from heaven. Satan then convinced humanity that he was god, an action that caused the true God to send Christ (a spirit who entered Mary through her ear); his mission was to enlighten humanity as to the ways of the devil and to reveal the truth about God. *The Vision of Isaiah* was accepted by both the moderate and absolute schools, as it "showed a material world and a firmament riven by the battle between Satanic and Godly forces."

The most important surviving Cathar tract is *The Book of the Two Principles*, which was written in the 1240s. The author was probably John of Lugio, a Cathar from the Albanensian school, which was part of the absolutist church of Desenzano. It has been described as "the most decisive evidence that the Cathars were evolving their own ideas about the nature of Dualism," and were not content simply to recycle Bogomil material. *The Book of the Two Principles* is a sustained attack on the moderate school, which the author regards as being little better than Catholicism. The work makes a case for there being two coeternal principles of good and evil, each of which created their own spheres—heaven and the material world respectively. The true god cannot be the author of evil. The verse in the Gospel of John which states "All

◀ According to the theology of dualist sects such as the Cathars and the Bogomils, the Devil was a force as real, and almost as powerful, as God himself.

things were made by it [the Word of God], and without it, was made nothing" was interpreted as meaning that "nothing"—that is, the material world—was made by Satan. The true world was the domain of the real creator god; this was not a world of matter, but a higher world with its own laws.

Also extant is a very late tract—possibly from the third quarter of the fourteenth century—called *The Vindication of the Church of God*. It presents the Cathars "as a persecuted and martyred church, suffering before the appearance of the Antichrist and the Last Judgment." It states that "this Church of God has received such power from our Lord Jesus Christ that sins are pardoned by its prayer;" that "this Church refrains from adultery;" that "this Church refrains from theft;" and concludes that "this Church keeps and observes all the commandments of the law of life," in sharp contrast to "the wicked Roman Church."

The Last Cathars

The last Cathars haunted the remote valleys of the Piedmont. Here they coexisted with groups of fugitive Waldensians, only occasionally breaking their cover, for example, to murder a priest who tipped off the Inquisition about their location in 1332, and to mete out the same treatment to two Inquisitors in 1365 and 1374. Once enemies, the Waldensians and the Cathars were now forced together by circumstance, and "came to see persecution as a special mark of the true church." The persecution continued in the form of sporadic military action, and slowly but surely, the Inquisition closed in on the last remaining communities. Antonio di Settimo di Savigliano's inquisition of 1387–1389 uncovered the last two major Cathars: Antonio di Galosna and Jacob Bech.

Di Galosna had been a Franciscan in Chieri, near Turin, but in 1362 he had been introduced to heresy at a house in Andezeno, a small town to the north-east of Chieri. The ceremony he participated in seems to have been part-Waldensian and part-Cathar, which indicates that, by this very late date, the Piedmont Cathars were practicing a hybrid form of the faith. This degenerate form of Catharism seems to have

▼ The valleys of Piedmont in Italy, one of the final redoubts of the long-suffering Cathar movement.

embraced some bizarre rituals. Antonio di Galosna's testimony states that at a certain point he was ritually struck on the head with a sword in order to induct him into the heresy. He was then given dualist instruction, in which God was extolled as the creator of heaven, but not of earth, the latter being the work of a fearsome dragon, which exercised more power in the earthly realm than the true god.

Jacob Bech's confession makes it clear that not all of the Piedmont Cathars entertained notions about dragons. He seems to have been instructed in the more orthodox Cathar view that material creation was under the sway of Satan. He also told the Inquisition of links between the Piedmont Cathars and Croatian Bogomils, who had apparently converted Bech to the faith, and who had their own pope. Savigliano also learned that, after a somewhat itinerant existence, Bech had settled in Chieri, where moderate Catharism was rife, and that a number of other Cathars had gone from there to Bosnia for further instruction. Both Galosna and Bech were, predictably, burned at the stake. Western Catharism died with them.

▲ The Waldenesians, who became allies of the Cathars, are shown fleeing from their persecutors.

By way of a postscript, the Inquisition returned to Chieri in 1412 and dug up 15 dead Cathars—some of whom had been named by Bech as having journeyed to Bosnia. They made a bonfire of the remains; there were apparently no living Cathars left to burn.

▶ Scenes from Wolfram's *Parzival*, the first German epic to take the Grail quest as its subject.

The Cathar Treasure

Since the demise of the Cathars, many legends have circulated about them. Most of these stories have centered on the so-called "Cathar treasure," which was said to have disappeared during the siege of Montségur, and on the relationship between the Cathars and the troubadours and the Knights Templar. While much of this speculation seems to be the result of the romanticization of the faith by writers such as Napoléon Peyrat (1809–1881) and Déodat Roché (1877–1978), such legends have actually been circulating since the 1320s at least. They have played a crucial role in shaping the mystique surrounding the Cathars, which in turn has gone a long way in helping to retain the interest and imagination of the public, of historians, and of generations of mystics.

Perhaps the most enduring myth about the Cathars is that they possessed the Holy Grail. The first published version of the Grail myth—*Le Conte du Graal*—was written in around 1180 by Chrétien de Troyes. It recounts the attempts of King Arthur's knights to find the Grail. Troyes died before he finished the story, so in this version the Grail is never found. The tale was picked up Wolfram von Eschenbach, whose name remains closely associated with the Grail story. Von Eschenbach's greatest work is *Parzival*, which is often understood to be a complex allegory of the path of spiritual development, and which betrays the influence of Eastern philosophy (Von Eschenbach is thought to have traveled to the East on a Crusade).

▼ An illustration from a fourteenth-century manuscript of *Le Conte du Graal* by Chrétien de Troyes, in which Perceval presents the Holy Grail to King Arthur.

▶ According to one of the Cathar inner teachings, Mary Magdalene was the wife of Jesus, a theory that has been revived in recent times.

He continued to write about the Grail in *Titurel*, and identified the Grail castle as being in the Pyrenees. Moreover, he described the lord of the Grail castle as being called "Perilla." The fact that Montségur is in the Pyrenees, and that its lord, Raymond Pereille, often signed his name in Latin, *Perilla*, has led to much speculation. Von Eschenbach's account has made it harder for historians to dismiss a connection between the Grail and the Cathars. It at least suggests that the Grail myth has been a part of the Cathar story since the time of the Good Christians, and is not just the invention of later writers.

▼ One theory holds that the Grail is not the cup used at the Last Supper, but the symbol of Christ's supposed nuptials at the "Wedding in Cana."

The Grail described in *Parzival* is a stone, and is reminiscent of the Stone of the Philosophers known to alchemy. However, there have been alternative interpretations of the Grail. It is often said to be the cup that Christ used at the Last Supper, and that later contained the blood he shed at Calvary. More controversially, it has been said

to represent the womb of Mary Magdalene, which received his seed after she married Jesus at Cana. One hypothesis holds that the Cathar treasure, which was smuggled out of Montségur shortly before the surrender, was in fact the Holy Grail, which was then either hidden in a nearby cave or entrusted to the Knights Templar. The sergeant of Montségur, Imbert of Salles, however, told the Inquisition that the Cathar treasure was merely money and precious stones. The Magdalene hypothesis suggests that the words Holy Grail, *san graal* in French, is in fact a misspelling of *sang real*, the "holy blood," meaning the bloodline of Jesus and Mary Magdalene. It was one of the Cathars' inner teachings, which was passed on only to the Perfect, that the Magdalene was Jesus's wife. This is puzzling since the Cathars despised marriage. Furthermore, this was not a belief inherited from the Bogomils. It is possible that the idea that Jesus and Mary Magdalene were married reflected a popular Languedocian tradition, but we cannot be certain.

The Troubadours and the Knights Templar

The two groups with whom the Cathars are most often associated are the troubadours and the Knights Templar, both of whom had a very strong presence in the Languedoc during the thirteenth century. The troubadours were itinerant poets, writing in Occitan, who flourished between the eleventh and thirteenth centuries. In Germany, their counterparts were known as the Minnesingers, and Wolfram von Eschenbach was one of their number.

▶ The troubadours often enjoyed the patronage of the very families who had supported and protected the Cathars in the Languedoc.

◄ Jacques de Molay, the last Grand Master of the Knights Templar and guardian of the fabled Templar treasure.

The troubadours' main themes were chivalry and courtly love. Some poems were literally love songs, often addressed to a woman who was unattainable, while other troubadour poems and songs were actually allegories of spiritual development, and betray an awareness of the Divine Feminine. Among the most celebrated troubadours were Peter Vidal, William Figueira, and Jaufré Rudel. In the Languedoc, they enjoyed the protection of the same families who protected the Cathars. At least one troubadour, William de Durfort, was known to be a Cathar; no doubt there were others. The concept of the Divine Feminine suggests another link between the two movements: The Perfect, upon being consoled, were given the title of *Theotokos*, which means God-Bearer, a turn of phrase that is more usually associated with the Virgin Mary.

▲ Knights Templar were brought before Philip IV of France and Pope Clement V and accused of many crimes. It now seems that none of the accusations were true.

▶ Philip IV of France led the persecution of the Knights Templar, hoping to seize their vast wealth.

The Knights Templar were the most powerful military religious order of their day, and were major landowners in the Languedoc. While theories suggesting that the Cathar treasure—whatever its nature—was entrusted to the Templars remain fanciful, there are a number of more definite links between the heretics and the soldier-monks. One of the Templars' great Grand Masters, Bertrand de Blancfort, came from a Cathar family, and during the Albigensian Crusade, the Templars welcomed fugitive Cathars into the order. In some Templar preceptories in the Languedoc, Cathars outnumbered Catholics.

Furthermore, the Templars refused to participate in the Albigensian Crusade. There could have been a number of reasons for this. They had a great deal of support in the Languedoc, so any military intervention there would have been politically disastrous for the order. Over and above these reasons, one cannot help but wonder if certain elements within the order remained sympathetic to the Cathars. This theory is rendered the more plausible by the fact that the Templars were themselves viciously suppressed between 1307 and 1312 on charges of heresy, blasphemy, and sodomy—accusations that had earlier been leveled against the Cathars.

The Persecuting Society

The Cathars emerged at a time of profound change in Europe. The historian R.I. Moore has argued that western society formed its institutions through the persecution of heretics and others in the thirteenth century. Furthermore, definitions of heresy played a large part in shaping the concept of witchcraft, which led to the persecution and execution of thousands of innocent people—predominantly women—during the witch hunts of the sixteenth and seventeenth centuries. It is perhaps the Cathars' quest for an authentic spirituality that makes their story still relevant.

▼ The Cathars' courage in the face of persecution, and their quest for a simple spirituality, are qualities that appeal to people in the modern world.

The Cathars' claim to be part of an authentic apostolic tradition dating back to the time of Christ cannot be proved. The Catholic Church's claim to descend from Peter is also, however, historically unverifiable. Something that perhaps finds in the Cathars' favor is one of the *Dead Sea Scrolls*, made public for the first time in 1991. It has been alleged that the end of the *Damascus Document— The Foundations of Righteousness: An Excommunication Text*—appears to show the excommunication of Paul from the Christian community. If this is indeed the case, then it would automatically invalidate the Catholic Church's claim to be God's vicars on earth, since most of the major forms of organized Christianity are based on the teachings of Paul, not Christ. The Church obviously feels that publication of the text has not damaged its position, and in May 2000 Pope John Paul II issued an apology for the Crusades. Many felt that the statement did not go far enough in offering rapprochement to the Arab world. No mention at all was made of the Albigensian Crusade. It remains unlikely that the papacy will ever apologize for that.

▲ In 2000, Pope John Paul II apologized for the Holy Land Crusades, but made no mention of the Albigensian Crusade or of the mass murder of Cathars.

It may be that the real Cathar treasure is to be found in their stress on simplicity, equality, nonviolence, work, and love. By not building churches, they somehow brought divinity into the domestic sphere. For the Cathars, spirituality was not an aspect of religious observance, it was something to be lived through every moment of every day.

Reference

Chronology

930s–940s	Emergence of Bogomilism in Bulgaria
c. 970	First anti-Bogomil tract, Cosmas the Priest's *Sermon Against the Heretics*
991	Gerbert d'Aurillac, later Pope Sylvester II, forced to swear his orthodoxy at Rheims
999	Leutard, first known heretic in the West, active in Châlons-sur-Marne
1022	First arrests and executions for heresy in the West, at Orléans
1082	Bogomil missionaries possibly active in Sicily
c. 1100	Execution of Bogomil Heresiarch, Basil the Physician, in Constantinople
1110s–1150s	Heretics at large: Era of Tanchelm of Antwerp, Arnold of Brescia, Henry of Lausanne
1143	First recorded mention of Cathars, burned at Cologne
1145	St Bernard preaches against Cathars and visits the Languedoc
1163	Council of Tours; Eckbert of Schönau's *Sermones ad Catharos*
1165	Cathar/Catholic debate at Lombers
1167	Cathar Conference at St Félix
1179	Third Lateran Council: Use of force against heretics recommended
1181	Shortlived military campaign against Cathars in Lavaur, led by Henri de Marcy
1184	*Ad abolendam* denounces the Cathars and other heretical sects
1198	Accession of Pope Innocent III; Cistercians appointed to preach to heretics in the Languedoc
1199	*Vergentis in senium* equates heresy with treason, and allows heretics' property to be confiscated
1203	April: Bosnian Church forced to swear fealty to Rome; Arnold Amaury and Peter of Castelnau appointed papal legates in the Languedoc
1204–1207	Cathar/Catholic debates in the Languedoc
1204	Refortification of Montségur

1206	March: Dominic de Guzmán proposes preaching in poverty in the Languedoc to bring people back to the Church; the Dominican Order is later founded as a result
1208	14 January: Assassination of Peter of Castelnau 10 March: Innocent calls for a Crusade against the Cathars
1209	18 June: Raymond VI publicly flogged 22 July: Sack of Béziers. At least 9,000 people murdered by Crusaders; start of the Albigensian Crusade Early August: Siege of Carcassonne 15 August: Surrender of Carcassonne Late August: Simon de Montfort becomes viscount of Béziers and Carcassonne, and assumes leadership of the Albigensian Crusade 10 November: Raymond Roger Trencavel found dead in his cell
1210	April: Siege and fall of Bram; forced march of 100 blinded and mutilated men to Cabaret; fall of Cabaret June/July: Siege and fall of Minerve 22 July: 140 Perfect burned outside Minerve
1212	April/May: Siege and fall of Lavaur; 80 knights hanged; Lady Geralda of Lavaur thrown down a well and stoned to death 3 May: 400 Perfect burned outside Lavaur Late May: 50–100 Perfect burned at Les Cassès
1213	17 January: Innocent suspends the Albigensian Crusade 21 May: Innocent persuaded to relaunch Crusade 12 September: Battle of Muret; King Peter II of Aragon killed; at least 7,000 die with him
1215	20 November: Fourth Lateran Council transfers land to Simon de Montfort, making him lord of all Languedoc
1216	16 July Innocent dies unexpectedly in Perugia August: Sack of Toulouse
1217	13 September: Soldiers loyal to Raymond VI enter Toulouse; siege of Toulouse begins
1218	25 June: Simon de Montfort killed outside walls of Toulouse
1219	Massacre of Marmande: 7,000 killed
1221	Death of St Dominic
1222	August: Death of Raymond VI
1224	Amaury de Montfort relinquishes control of the Languedoc to the French crown
1225	Death of Arnold Amaury

1226	Spring: Louis VIII's Crusade against the South gets underway Cathar Council of Pieusse: Bishopric of the Razès founded 8 November: Louis dies at 39; his widow, Blanche of Castile, becomes Regent
1228	Scorched-earth campaign against Toulouse
1229	12 April: Raymond VII publicly flogged in Paris; end of the Albigensian Crusade
1233	Spring: Inquisition founded to combat Catharism 30 July: First Inquisitor Conrad Tors murdered August: 200 Cathars and Waldensians burned in Verona
1234–1246	Crusades against heresy in Bosnia
1239	180 heretics burned at Mont Aimé in Champagne
1240	Trencavel Revolt
1240s	*The Book of the Two Principles* thought to have been written
1242	28 May: Inquisitors Stephen of St Thibéry and William Arnold murdered at Avignonet; Raymond VII launches final campaign against the Papacy and French crown
1243	May: Siege of Montségur begins
1244	2 March: Montségur surrenders on condition of a two-week truce 13 March: 21 Believers and mercenaries ask for—and are given—the *consolamentum* 16 March: Montségur evacuated; all 225 Perfect are burned on the so-called Field of the Cremated
1245–1246	Extensive Inquisitorial proceedings in the Languedoc
1249	June: Raymond VII burns 80 Cathars at Agen September: Death of Raymond VII
1252	Inquisitor Peter of Verona (St. Peter Martyr) murdered in Italy; use of torture given papal approval by Innocent VI
1255	August: Fall of Quéribus, last Cathar stronghold in the Languedoc
1276	Fall of Sirmione, last Cathar fortress in Italy
1278	February: Burning of more than 200 Perfect in Verona
1296	October: Peter and William Autier travel to Lombardy to be consoled

1299	Autumn: Autiers return to the Languedoc: Start of Cathar revival
1305	September: William Bélibaste's first encounter with Autier Perfect while in hiding after murdering a fellow shepherd
1303	Appointment of Geoffrey d'Ablis as Inquisitor in Carcassonne
1307	Appointment of Geoffrey d'Ablis as Inquisitor in Toulouse September: Bélibaste, imprisoned for heresy, escapes from jail
1308	8 September: Entire village of Montaillou arrested on heresy charges
1309	Late summer: Peter Autier arrested
1310	9 April: Autier burned at the stake in Toulouse
1315	Bélibaste establishes Cathar community in Morella and Sant Mateu, south of Tarragona in Catalonia
1317	James Fournier becomes bishop of Pamiers and begins Inquisitorial proceedings
1321	March: Bélibaste betrayed and arrested Last known Italian Cathar bishop arrested
1325	Pope John XXII calls for action against the Bosnian Church
1329	16 January: Peter Clergue, rector of Montaillou, posthumously burned
1342	Last known Cathar in Florence appears before the Inquisition
1387–1389	Inquisition of Antonio di Settimo di Savigliano. Antonio di Galosna and Jacob Bech arrested and burned
1412	Posthumous burning of 15 Cathars at Chieri
1459	Bosnian Church persecuted by King Stephen Thomas
1463	Fall of Bosnia to the Ottoman Turks
1867	Last reported Bogomils in Bosnia

Glossary

Adoptionism Belief that Christ was not born divine, but only became so after his baptism.

Apparellamentum Monthly rite of confession performed by the Perfect, who would usually confess to a Cathar deacon, or, occasionally, a bishop.

Arianism Named after Arius (256–336), a Christian priest from Alexandria, who denied that Christ and God were one person, seeing them instead as two different Divine entities. The heresy was the first serious doctrinal dispute the Church had to face once it had been legalized by Constantine, and it was the major issue faced by the Council of Nicea.

Believers The majority of Cathars were Believers. That is to say, they had taken the *convenanza*, but were not yet consoled. They were not subject to any dietary restrictions.

Bogomilism Dualist heresy founded by the priest Bogomil in the early tenth century. It appears to have influenced Catharism strongly, although the earliest tangible evidence is only datable to 1167. The movement considerably outlived the Cathars, with reports of Bogomils continuing up to the nineteenth century.

Celtic church According to tradition, the Celtic church was founded by Joseph of Arimathea at Glastonbury during the mid-first century A.D., and the case could be made for the Celtic church being the original form of Christianity in Europe. It went into decline after the Synod of Whitby in 664, where it was forcibly absorbed into the Catholic Church. Numerous modern Celtic churches exist today.

Consolamentum Cathar rite of baptism that elevated the Believer to the state of a Perfect. Many Cathars took the *consolamentum* on their deathbeds.

Convenanza Formal rite that made a Cathar Listener a Believer.

Docetism The belief that Christ did not have a physical body, common amongst Gnostics. Docetics believed that Jesus's body was an illusion, as was his Crucifixion. Docetism was declared heretical by the Church. Both the Bogomils and the Cathars were Docetist.

Donatism Heresy that denied the validity of offices said by corrupt priests. Many of the reform movements of the eleventh and twelfth centuries were sympathetic to the Donatist position. The Cathars were Donatist in that a *consolamentum* performed by a Perfect who later—even accidentally—broke their vows was invalid.

Dualism The belief that good and evil are two independent, opposing principles. Absolute dualists regard the evil principle to be as strong as the good, and see the two as being locked in conflict for all time. Absolute dualists frequently regard time as cyclical and believe in reincarnation. Moderate dualists see evil as being inferior to the good principle, which will triumph over it at the end of time. Both maintain a hostility to the material world. The Cathars began as moderates, but were converted to absolute dualism at the Council of St Félix. Some Cathars, such as the Church of Concorezzo, remained moderates.

Essenes Radical Jewish sect that existed from the second century B.C. to the first century A.D. Arguments have been put forward to suggest that both Jesus and John the Baptist had links with the sect. The community at Qumran, which produced the *Dead Sea Scrolls*, is thought to have been Essene.

Elchasaites Jewish Christian sect who were, interestingly, also known as *katharoi*. Their most famous member was the Persian prophet Mani.

Endura Cathar rite that allows the newly consoled nothing but cold water. Mainly associated with the Autier revival—when it was a practical necessity—the *endura* was in fact a feature of Catharism from the beginning.

Gnostic Term used to designate many different sects who flourished in the first few centuries A.D. Although nominally Christian, many elements of Gnosticism are pre-Christian, such as the belief in dualism. The name derives from the Greek word for knowledge, *gnosis*.

Listeners In the Cathar context, a Listener was a person was interested in Catharism, but was not ready or willing to become an actual member of the church, which required the taking of the *convenanza*.

Manicheism Universalist, dualist religion founded by the Persian prophet Mani (A.D. 216–275). It was seen as the worst heresy since Marcionism (see below), and St. Augustine—once a member of the sect—denounced it. It was largely wiped out in Europe during the sixth century, although it survived for another thousand years in Asia. "Manichean" became a byword for heretic during the Middle Ages.

Marcionism Gnostic dualist sect that taught the principle of the two gods, with Christ being the son of the true god, and the Jehovah of the Old Testament being seen as the evil god.

Massalianism Dualist heresy that is thought to have originated in fourth-century Mesopotamia. The name means "the praying people." Also known as Enthusiasts.

Melioramentum Formal greeting made by a Cathar Believer to a Perfect.

Nestorianism The belief, first proposed by Nestorius (c. 386–c. 451), the patriarch of Constantinople, that Christ's person contained two separate beings, one human, the other divine. Nestorianism was declared heretical at the Council of Ephesus in 431, but the Nestorian church—despite persecution—survives to this day.

Patarenes Italian name for Cathars. The term was also used in Bosnia.

Paulicianism Dualist heresy that emerged in seventh-century Armenia. In 717, a council of the Armenian Church denounced them as "sons of Satan" and "fuel for the fire eternal." They are thought to have survived until the seventeenth century.

Pelagianism Pelagius (c. 360–c. 435) was a British monk whose teachings denied Original Sin. Pelagianism was condemned as heresy at the Council of Carthage in 417.

Perfect The Cathar equivalent of priests, they were austere black-robed ascetics who were the heart and soul of the Cathar movement. Bogomilism also had Perfect.

Piphles According to Eckbert of Schönau, this was the name used for dualist heretics in Flanders, but no one knows where the word came from.

Publicans Name used for heretics in the twelfth century, a group of whom came to England to proselytise during the reign of Henry II.

Texerant According to Eckbert of Schönau, this was the name used for dualist heretics in France. The name derives from the word for weaving, a craft long associated with heresy.

Waldensians Founded by the preacher Waldo of Lyons (1140–1217), the group espoused evangelical poverty and was also known as the Poor of Lyons as a result. They were declared heretical in the bull *Ad abolendam* in 1184—which also denounced the Cathars. Despite persecution, the Waldensian church survives to this day.

Suggestions for Further Reading

The most comprehensive recent book on the Cathars in English is Malcolm Lambert's *The Cathars* (Blackwell, 1998). As a slightly easier read, Malcolm Barber's *The Cathars: Dualist Heretics in Languedoc in the High Middle Ages* (Longman, 2000) is also recommended. Stephen O'Shea's *The Perfect Heresy: The Life and Death of the Cathars* (Profile Books, 2000) is perhaps the best nonacademic introduction to the Cathars, although the book mainly concentrates on events in the Languedoc (although it does come with copious—and frequently entertaining—endnotes).

Late Catharism is most famously represented by Emmanuel Le Roy Ladurie's *Montaillou* (Paris, 1975; English edition, 1980). More recently, René Weis's brilliant *The Yellow Cross: The Story of the Last Cathars 1290–1329* (Penguin, 2001) has covered the same ground in painstaking and moving detail.

Older classics on the subject include Sir Steven Runciman's *The Medieval Manichee* (1947) and Zoé Oldenburg's *Massacre at Montségur* (1959).

For actual Cathar texts, the best source remains *Heresies of the High Middle Ages*, edited by Wakefield and Evans (Columbia University Press, 1969).

The two major contemporary accounts of the Albigensian Crusade are: *The Song of the Cathar Wars: A History of the Albigensian Crusade* by William of Tudela and an anonymous successor, translated by Janet Shirley (Scolar Press, 1996) and *The History of the Albigensian*

Crusade: Peter of les Vaux-de-Cernay's Historia Albigensis, translated by W.A. and M.D. Sibly (Boydell, 1998).

In addition to these titles, the curious reader is directed toward the works of Anne Brenon, Jean Duvernoy, Bernard Hamilton and Michel Roquebert, all of whom are major authorities on Catharism. For the history of dualism, one should look no further than Yuri Stoyanov's masterly *The Other God* (Yale University Press, 2000), the first edition of which was published as *The Hidden Tradition in Europe* (Penguin Books, 1994).

With regard to early Christianity, John Davidson's *The Gospel of Jesus: In Search of His Original Teachings* (Element Books, 1995) is a benchmark in the field, as is Robert Eisenman's *James, the Brother of Jesus* (Faber and Faber, 1997).

Finally, I would like to recommend the works of Arthur Guirdham, in particular his *The Cathars and Reincarnation* (Neville Spearman, 1970) and *The Great Heresy: The History and Beliefs of the Cathars* (Neville Spearman, 1977). And for the adventurous, there is always Chris Ratcliffe and Elaine Connell's *Cycling in Search of the Cathars* (Pennine Pens, 1990).

Select Bibliography

The Cathars

Arnold, John H., *Inquisition and Power: Catharism and the Confessing Subject in Medieval Languedoc* University of Pennsylvania Press, 2001

Barber, Malcolm, *The Cathars: Dualist Heretics in Languedoc in the High Middle Ages* Longman, 2000

Birks, Walter, and Gilbert, R.A., *The Treasure of Montségur: A Study of the Cathar Heresy and the Nature of the Cathar Secret* Crucible, 1987

Brenon, Anne, *Le Vrai Visage du Catharisme* Loubatieres, 1988; *Les Femmes Cathares* Perrin, 1992

Cartner, George, *Flames of Faith: The Cathars of the Languedoc* B & C Press, 2003

Costen, Michael, *The Cathars and the Albigensian Crusade* Manchester University Press, 1997

Dutton, Claire, *Aspects of the Institutional History of the Albigensian Crusades 1198–1229* Royal Holloway and Bedford New College, University of London, 1993 (PhD Thesis)

Duvernoy, Jean, *Le Catharisme* (2 Vols) Privat, 1976/1979

Fichtenau, Heinrich, *Heretics and Scholars in the High Middle Ages 1000–1200* Pennsylvania State University Press, 1998

Gordon, James, *The Laity and the Catholic Church in Cathar Languedoc* Oxford PhD Thesis, 1992

Guirdham, Arthur, *The Great Heresy: The History and Beliefs of the Cathars* C.W. Daniel, 1993

Hamilton, Bernard, *The Albigensian Crusade* Historical Association, 1974; *Monastic Reform, Catharism and the Crusades (900–1300)* Variorum, 1979; *Crusaders, Cathars and the Holy Places* Ashgate/Variorum, 2000

Lambert, Malcolm, *The Cathars* Blackwell, 1998

Lansing, Carol, *Power & Purity: Cathar Heresy in Medieval Italy* Oxford University Press, 1998

Mundy, John Hine, *The Repression of Catharism at Toulouse: The Royal Diploma of 1279* Pontifical Institute of Mediaeval Studies, 1985; *Men and Women at Toulouse in the Age of the Cathars* Pontifical Institute of Mediaeval Studies, 1990

Markale, Jean, *Montségur and the Mystery of the Cathars* Inner Traditions, 2003

Oldenbourg, Zoé, *Massacre at Montségur: A History of the Albigensian Crusade* Phoenix, 1998

O'Shea, Stephen, *The Perfect Heresy: The Revolutionary Life and Death of the Medieval Cathars* Profile Books, 2000

Rahn, Otto, *Kreuzzug gegen den Gral. Die Tragödie des Katharismus* Stuttgart, 1964

Ratcliffe, Chris, and Connell, Elaine, *Cycling in Search of the Cathars* Pennine Pens, 1990

Roach, Andrew, *The Relationship of the Italian and Southern French Cathars, 1170–1320* University of Oxford, 1989 (PhD Thesis)

Roché, Déodat, *Le Catharisme* Toulouse, 1947; *L'Église romaine et les cathares albigeois* Éditions Cahiers d'études cathares, 1969

Ladurie, Emmanuel Le Roy, *Montaillou* Penguin, 1980

Roquebert, Michel, *L'Epopée cathare* (5 Vols) Privat/Perrin, 1970–1998

Roquette, Yves, *Cathars* Loubatieres, 1992

Sumption, Jonathan, *The Albigensian Crusades* Faber and Faber, 1978

Strayer, Joseph R. with a new epilogue by Carol Lansing *The Albigensian Crusades* University of Michigan Press, 1992

Wakefield, W.L., *Heresy, Crusade and Inquisition in Southern France, 1100–1250*

Allen and Unwin, 1974

Weis, René, *The Yellow Cross* Penguin, 2001

Contemporaneous Accounts and Sources

Hamilton, Janet and Hamilton, Bernard (Editors/Translators) with the assistance of Yuri Stoyanov (Translator), *Christian Dualist Heresies in the Byzantine World, c. 650–c. 1450: Selected Sources* Manchester University Press, 1998

Shirley, Janet (Translator), *The Song of the Cathar Wars: A History of the Albigensian Crusade by William of Tudela and an anonymous successor* Scolar Press, 1996

Sibly, W.A. and Sibly, M.D. (Translators), *The History of the Albigensian Crusade: Peter of les Vaux-de-Cernay's Historia Albigensis* Boydell, 1998

Wakefield, W.L. and Evans, Austin P. (Editors) *Heresies of the High Middle Ages Columbia* University Press, 1991

Selections from James Fournier's Inquisition proceedings have been translated by Nancy P. Stork and can be viewed online at the website of San José State University, http://www.sjsu.edu/. Search for "Fournier register" on the home page to find the current location of the pages.

Heresy

Biller, Peter and Hudson, Anne (Editors), *Heresy and Literacy, 1000–1530* Cambridge University Press, 1994

George, Leonard, *The Encyclopedia of Heresies and Heretics* Robson Books, 1995

Lambert, Malcolm, *Medieval Heresy: Popular Movements from the Gregorian Reform to the Reformation* Blackwell, 2002

Runciman, Sir Steven, *The Medieval Manichee* Cambridge University Press, 1947

Stoyanov, Yuri, *The Other God: Dualist Religions from Antiquity to the Cathar Heresy* Yale University Press, 2000

Early Christianity

Baigent, Michael and Leigh, Richard, *The Dead Sea Scrolls Deception* Arrow Books, 2001

Davidson, John, *The Gospel of Jesus: In Search of His Original Teachings* Element, 1995

Eisenman, Robert, *James, the Brother of Jesus* Faber, 1997; *The Dead Sea Scrolls Uncovered* (with Michael Wise), Penguin, 1992

Elliott, J.K. and James, M.R. (Editors), *The Apocryphal New Testament* Oxford University Press, 1993

Kersten, Holger, *Jesus Lived in India* Element, 1986

Miller, Robert J. (Editor), *The Complete Gospels* HarperCollins, 1994

Pagels, Elaine, *The Gnostic Gospels* Penguin, 1982

Robinson, James M. (Editor), *The Nag Hammadi Library in English* HarperCollins, 1990

Sparks, H.F.D. (Editor), *The Apocryphal Old Testament* Oxford University Press, 1984

Vermes, Geza (Translator/Editor), *The Complete Dead Sea Scrolls in English* Penguin, 2004

Wilson, A.N., *Paul: The Mind of the Apostle* Sinclair-Stevenson, 1997

Satanology

Pagels, Elaine, *Adam Eve and the Serpent* Penguin, 1990; *The Origin of Satan* Allen Lane, 1996

Russell, Jeffrey Burton, *Satan: The Early Christian Tradition* Cornell University Press, 1981; *Lucifer: The Devil in the Middle Ages* Cornell University Press, 1984

Related Interest

Anderson, William, *Dante the Maker* Routledge & Kegan Paul, 1980

Angebert, Jean-Michel *The Occult and the Third Reich* Macmillan, 1974

Angelov, Dimiter, *The Bogomil Movement* Sofia Press, 1987

Armstrong, T.J., *Cecilia's Vision* Headline, 2001

Baigent, Michael, Leigh, Richard and Lincoln, Henry, *The Holy Blood and the Holy Grail* Corgi, 1983

Baigent, Michael and Leigh, Richard, *The Inquisition* Penguin, 2000

Bihalji-Merin, O. and Benac, Alojz, with photographs by Toso Dabac, *The Bogomils* Thames & Hudson, 1962

Cohn, Norman, *The Pursuit of the Millennium* Pimlico, 1993; *Europe's Inner Demons: The Demonisation of Christians in Medieval Christendom* Pimlico, 1993

Dick, Philip K., *VALIS* Vintage Books, 1991

Fine Jr, J.V.A., "The Bosnian Church: A New Interpretation," *East European Quarterly*, 1975

Frayling, Christopher, *Strange Landscape: A Journey through the Middle Ages* Penguin, 1996

Garsoïan, Nina G., *The Paulician Heresy* Mouton & Co, 1967

Ginzburg, Carlo, *The Cheese and the Worms: The Cosmos of a 16th Century Miller* Penguin, 1992

Godwin, Malcolm, *The Holy Grail: Its Origins, Secrets & Meaning Revealed* Bloomsbury, 1994

Guirdham, Arthur, *The Cathars and Reincarnation* C. W. Daniel, 1990; *We are One Another* C.W. Daniel, 1991; *The Lake and the Castle* C.W. Daniel, 1991; *A Foot in Both Worlds* C.W. Daniel, 1991

Holroyd, Stuart, *The Elements of Gnosticism* Element, 1994

Levack, Brian P., *The Witch-Hunt in Early Modern Europe* Longman, 1995

Martin, Lois, *The History of Witchcraft* Pocket Essentials, 2002

Martin, Sean, *The Knights Templar* Pocket Essentials, 2004

Moore, R.I., *The Formation of a Persecuting Society: Power and Deviance in Western Europe, 950–1250* Blackwell, 1987

Obolensky, Dmitri, *The Bogomils: A Study in Balkan Neo-Manichaeism* Cambridge University Press, 1948

Panichas, George (Editor), *The Simone Weil Reader* Moyer Bell, 1977

Picknett, Lynne, and Prince, Clive, *The Templar Revelation* Bantam, 1997

Richards, Jeffrey, *Sex, Dissidence and Damnation: Minority Groups in the Middle Ages* Routledge, 1990

Sharenkov, Viktor N., *A Study of Manichaeism in Bulgaria, with special reference to the Bogomils* New York, 1927

Tashkovski, Dragan, *Bogomilism in Macedonia* Macedonian Review Editions, 1975

Tuchman, Barbara W., *A Distant Mirror: The Calamitous Fourteenth Century* Macmillan, 1992

Index